D0270202

Greek Vegetarian Cookery

4

000000348

By the same author

Indian Vegetarian Cookery
Indian Meat and Fish Cookery
Anna Yoga: The Yoga of Food
Indian Sweet Cookery
Chinese Vegetarian Cookery

Greek Vegetarian Cookery

Jack Santa Maria

Illustrated by Kate Simunek

Rider

London Melbourne Sydney Auckland Johannesburg

Rider & Company

An imprint of the Hutchinson Publishing Group

17–21 Conway Street, London W 1 P 6 J D

Hutchinson Publishing Group (Australia) Pty Ltd
P O Box 496, 16–22 Church Street, Hawthorne, Melbourne,
Victoria 3122

Hutchinson Group (N Z) Ltd
32–34 View Road, P O Box 40–086, Glenfield, Auckland 10

Hutchinson Group (S A) Pty Ltd
P O Box 337, Bergvlei 2012, South Africa

First published 1984

© Jack Santa Maria 1984
Illustrations © Kate Simunek 1984

This book is sold subject to the condition that it shall
not by way of trade or otherwise be lent, resold,
hired out or otherwise circulated without the
publisher's prior consent in any form of binding other
than that in which it is published and without a
similar condition including this condition being
imposed on the subsequent purchaser

Set in Linotron Bembo by
Wyvern Typesetting Ltd, Bristol

Printed and bound in Great Britain by Anchor Brendon Ltd,
Tiptree, Essex

British Library Cataloguing in Publication Data
Santa Maria, Jack
  Greek vegetarian cookery
  1. Vegetarian cookery
  2. Cookery, Greek
  I. Title
641.5'636'09495   TX837
ISBN 0 09 155361 X

I at last realized that eating was a spiritual function . . .
THE NARRATOR, *Zorba the Greek*
BY NIKOS KAZANTZAKIS

Contents

Acknowlededgments

The author would like to thank many Greek friends and cooks for their help, especially Angela Fassoulis, the Vergadis family, Dimitri and Dimetra Voukalis, Margaret Rooney for her recipes and invaluable help during my travels in Greece and in testing many of the dishes herein, Diana and Peter Goff for their help and enthusiasm, and Geoffrey Chesler, my editor, for his help and encouragement.

The author would also like to thank Messrs Faber & Faber and Messrs Simon & Schuster for their permission to quote from *Zorba the Greek* by Nikos Kazantzakis, translated into English by Carl Wilder and published in London by Faber & Faber and in New York by Simon & Schuster.

Introduction

Life is short, a craft so long to learn.
HIPPOCRATES, *Aphorisms I.i.*

The writer of the Hippocratic treatise indicates that ancient medicine evolved ·from the discoveries made by cooks. Like the ancient Chinese, they noticed that sick people either went off their food altogether or they preferred other food or flavours. Cookery, therefore, played an important part in helping the sick person back to recovery and in improving health. So it is that the healing and health-promoting properties of vegetables, fruits and herbs are well recorded.

Homeric records (*c.* 800 BC) show that the Greeks have enjoyed cereals, fruits and vegetables since classical times and today Greece is even more a land of Mediterranean fragrance, tangy herbs and juicy fruits and vegetables. No other country is so essentially Mediterranean and this book aims to bring the essence of Mediterranean taste, aroma, colour and texture into the modern vegetarian kitchen.

Food in classical Greece was mainly based on corn, wine and oil, as it still is for many today. Wheat was made into bread and barley was made into porridge with milk and oil or honey. Cakes were made from various flours. Milk from sheep or goats was made into butter, cheese and yogurt. Meat was hardly eaten by ordinary folk except during festivals when an animal might be sacrificed. Peas, beans, dried legumes, onions, leeks and garlic were stewed with a few green vegetables and wild herbs. Potatoes and tomatoes were still waiting to be discovered in the Americas 2000 years later.

In the sixth century BC, Pythagoras, the great philosopher and mathematician, established a brotherhood at Crotone in southern Italy which was then part of the Greek world. In Sicily a temple still stands erected to Adephagia, the goddess of good eating and merrymaking. By the fifth century BC, figs, grapes, apples and pears were grown, but citrus fruits, cherries, peaches and apricots were as yet unknown in Greece. Honey was the most common sweetener, while salt and herbs were used for seasoning. Wine, often spiced, sweetened or drunk with water, was the most popular drink. Greeks have always made tea from wild flowers and herbs and they did not drink coffee until their contact with Arab merchants.

The philosopher Plato (*c.* 427–347 BC) was thought to be a vegetarian, though many Athenians in his day ate very little meat. In a famous discourse, Plato (calling himself after his teacher Socrates) gives a graphic picture of country fare at that time. In a discussion with his brothers Glaucon and Adeimantos, he describes the necessities of life which would be needed by the ordinary citizen of his ideal republic. For their nourishment, says Socrates, they will make barley meal and wheat flour from which they can prepare cakes and bread. These will be served on beds of reeds or leaves. Then, reclining on rough couches covered with bryony and myrtle flowers, they will feast with their families, drinking wine and singing to the gods. Glaucon interrupts, reminding Socrates that the people are supposed to be feasting. What goes with the bread? he asks. Of course, Socrates adds, they will have salt, olives, cheese, onions and greens, and the sort of things they boil up in the country (no doubt referring to herbs and other vegetables). For dessert they will have figs, chick peas and beans (with honey), roasted myrtleberries and chestnuts washed down with wine or herb tea (*The Republic 2. 12–13*).

Plato seems to be hinting that something more sophisticated was happening in the kitchens of aristocratic Athenians. Indeed, records show that, from the time of Alexander the Great (third century BC), talented cooks were in demand in the homes of the nobility. These cooks travelled widely so that their techniques also became known throughout Italy, North Africa and Asia Minor.

There were two main meals, as in Greece today, which were lunch and supper. Before work began at dawn, the household ate bread dipped in oil and drank a little wine. Lunch might include bread, pasta, vegetables and eggs and was an important meal. According to the Greek general and historian Xenophon (431–355 BC), Greek commanders had trouble getting their men to fight after lunch. Anyone who knows the effects of eating a hearty meal in the middle of the day in Greece would find this easy to understand.

Today the staple diet in the village is still dark bread which is baked at home, in a communal oven, or at the local baker's. For breakfast there is bread, cheese, yogurt, honey, olives and eggs with coffee, tea, or hot milk. The midday meal is the largest and most elaborate when the cities shut down for a four-hour break. This may consist of soup, salads, a main dish with bread, and fresh fruit. Supper or the evening meal is often a thick soup or stew with bread and fruit. Sweets and pastries are eaten between meals with a cup of coffee or glass of water. Eating customs may be different in the countryside with the largest meal served in the evening after the day's work in the fields. Two or three dishes are served in large earthenware bowls for everybody to serve themselves from. You sit at a low table with low seats or cushions and the meal is accompanied by olives and thick slices of wholemeal bread. Children have water from a pitcher and the grown-ups have wine in jugs or plain bottles drawn from the house supply.

The Greek village cook uses wholemeal flour which is rich in vitamins and essential fibre; olive oil, the most unsaturated of all the cooking fats; lemons, rich in vitamin C; fresh fruits and vegetables, rich in vitamins, minerals, fibre and natural sugars; fresh and dried legumes which are especially rich in protein; nuts and seeds, rich in protein and vegetable fats; yogurt and cheese made from sheep's and goat's milk – products which have been shown to be more beneficial to those suffering from sinus trouble, certain skin allergies and asthma, than cow's milk; and wild herbs for both seasoning and salads. With these simple but wholesome ingredients, Greek vegetarian cookery offers tasty and nourishing dishes which will improve and enrich your diet while broadening your vegetarian repertoire. *Kalí óreksi (bon appétit)!*

The Historical Background to Greek Cookery

There are historical reasons why Greek cookery is far less conservative than either French or Italian. The modern cuisine shows a willingness to change and adapt which reflects Greece's heroic survival as a nation through a turbulent history.

Although it is known as the 'cradle' of Western culture, neither in ancient times, nor in later centuries was there a country which could be termed 'Greece'. Rather, the history of what has now become the republic of Greece (*Ellás*) is the history of particular cities or regions. From the third millenium to about 1200 BC, after the migration of Indo-Europeans into Greece, a number of cultures existed on the mainland and islands. The best known of these is the Minoan culture of Crete. After the collapse of the Minoan Empire around 1400 BC, various city states evolved which fought for supremacy in the area. But the defeat of Xerxes the Persian in 480 BC brought a sense of ethnic and cultural identity to the Greeks. For a time the city of Athens gained control and both the arts and sciences flourished in spite of continual wars and the growing power of Sparta. The Macedonians (northern Greeks) defeated Athens in 338 BC and, sixty-three years after the death of Socrates (336 BC), Alexander founded the Macedonian world empire. This was not to last for long and Greece became the Roman province of Macedonia in 146 BC, remaining under Roman rule for five centuries.

At this time much of the Greek cuisine was assimilated by the Romans. Emperor Constantine proclaimed Christianity the official state religion and set up a new capital at Byzantium which he renamed Constantinople (AD 330). But by AD 393, when the last Olympic Games of antiquity took place, the Western Roman Empire was collapsing, and for the next thousand years the Byzantine Empire suffered a series of barbarian invasions. Later, as Europe threw off the shackles of barbarism, new city states emerged which looked towards Greece for plunder. Italians under Orsini seized the islands of Kefallinia, Ithaca and Zakinthos and, from the beginning of the thirteenth century, the Venetians occupied various parts of Greece, including Crete. Meanwhile, French armies, under the guise of a fourth religious crusade against the Muslims, took Constantinople and founded an Eastern Roman Empire in 1204. The Pope of Rome proceeded to divide up the world and allot portions of it, including Greece, to the European armies which were loyal to him. However, on 29 May 1453, Mehmet II of Turkey took Constantinople and so began 400 years of Turkish occupation until 1828. From then until after the Second World War, Greece suffered further occupation by Italy, Germany and Turkey.

During the last 1900 years of oppression, the Greek Orthodox Church has helped to preserve the national awareness of the Greeks and much of national life follows the pattern of religious festivals according to the Orthodox calendar – in fact it would seem impoverished without it. The other bastion of Greek life is the spoken and written language.

How has Greek cookery survived this historical process? There is a cuisine which can be regarded as Balkan and there is also one which is distinctly Turkish. At first sight it would appear that Greek cookery must be a combination of the two, with elements of other European influences thrown in, but that would be a simplification. During the 400-year Muslim rule of the Ottomans, the Greeks were forced to rename their dishes (and many other things) in Turkish for the benefit of the occupying forces. This has led to the erroneous assumption that most Greek dishes are Turkish in origin. Such influences are all too apparent, especially in restaurants. The kebab, for example, can be found anywhere from Greece and Turkey to northern India. But in the homes of the country people, on the islands and on the mainland, a distinctive Greek cuisine can be discovered which has been preserved intact. Its quality of simplicity has made it easy to overlook.

In the preparation of vegetarian dishes, the Greeks have much to offer the cook who is looking for a subtle blend of the Mediterranean and the Oriental. Here, are dainty pastries with savoury and sweet fillings; the use of wild plants in salads; delicate cheeses and yogurt made from sheep's and goat's milk; honey and sesame in sweets which are more like meals; full-bodied wines, some aromatized with pine resin or herbs; and, above all, the sunny tastes and textures of good bread, olives, olive oil, lemons, garlic and wild Mediterranean herbs.

Utensils and Serving

Before you enter a Greek village house, you may discover that some of the kitchen is outside or at least partly exposed. The scene has hardly changed since classical times. Here is the fire for cooking on, a stone sink for washing and cleaning vegetables, and an oven, often at eye-level, with an iron door. Near the fire is a clay cooking pot (*tsúka*) for making soups and stews. Inside the oven might be a copper baking pan (*tapsí*) which is lined with tin. The kitchen room is shady and cool. Here foodstuffs are stored and some of the more laborious cooking tasks are carried out. On the floor is a clay pitcher (*stámna*) for carrying water with perhaps a water ladle (*aklúmbi*) made from a gourd. A large clay jar (*pithári*) for storing oil stands in a corner and, leaning against the lime-washed wall, a long wooden paddle (*kopanáki*) which is used for shelling dried peas and beans. Near the olive-oil jar is a sealed crock (*píthos*) which contains last season's pickled vegetables. Wooden tools and pots are kept neatly in drawers and on shelves, and there, near the bunches of dried herbs, gleams that essential to Greek coffee-making – the *bríki*. This one is brass, but it could have been made of tinned copper or aluminium.

The modern cook needs no special utensils for Greek vegetarian cookery. A good set of pans, iron if possible, should be in every kitchen; a selection of wooden spoons and some metal spatulas, ladles and sieves; a good cutting knife and a wooden chopping board for vegetables; a large wooden board and rolling pin for kneading dough, rolling out pastry and for making up pastries and rolls with *fíllo* pastry; a good metal colander for straining vegetables; a pestle and mortar for grinding; and some good mixing bowls, jugs and metal baking tins, for making bread, cakes and sweets. The one utensil that you may like to purchase is a *bríki* for making Greek coffee (see Greek Coffee, p. 153). You may like to use a second chopping board for fruit and nuts since onions and garlic do seem to penetrate wood even when the board is washed with cold soapy water. It is a good plan to use separate wooden spoons for sweet and savoury cooking for the same reason.

Remember not to leave metal spoons in lemon juice or wine vinegar unless they are stainless.

You can serve your dishes in the usual way or you could try the Greek way of putting them all on the table and letting everyone help himself. This is a very pleasant way of eating, especially with a group of friends. If you intend to make a meal of *mezédhes* (see Appetizers, pp. 37–45), which should be a series of small dishes served with drinks, bring them to the table a few at a time.

Greek meals should be unhurried affairs. Allow plenty of time for conversation and for drinks before you begin the serious eating. Provide *orektiká* (appetizers) with your apéritifs which should ideally include ouzo. A typical meal could start with a selection of dips with bread, followed by a light soup. A main dish could be one of rice, pasta, beans or a stew, with a salad. Try to serve Greek, Cypriot or good full-bodied wine with the main course. Finish with some fresh fruit. Have a gap for more conversation or entertainment, then serve coffee and Greek brandy or a liqueur with pastries or sweets. If the food must be handled during the meal, provide some warm water in bowls with a drop of lemon juice, orange blossom water or rosewater for rinsing the hands. A posy of flowers in the centre of the table will complete the setting.

Flavour – The Herbs and Spices Shelf

Greeks like to use herbs which they have either grown or collected themselves. If you do not already have one, it would be a good plan to start a herb garden or herb window box. Look for common herbs when you are out in the country, especially when abroad in those countries which border the Mediterranean. You may see them at a time of the year when they are not ready for gathering, but at least you will gain some insight into the life of the plant whose dried, shredded and packeted leaves you may only come across in your local store. If a Greek wants you to test a herb the chances are that it will be rolled between warm fingers or palms for you to sniff, for it is true that what is described as the taste or flavour of food is mainly its aroma.

The tastes actually discerned in the mouth are sweet, sour, salt, alkaline or metallic, pungent or chilli-hot, bitter or astringent. Before adding herbs or spices to contribute aroma then, we must make sure that the true tastes of a dish are adjusted and we need to know what happens to them with a change of temperature.

Cold reduces sweet and sour tastes. Sweet wines, for example, taste less sweet when chilled. Retsina always tastes better chilled and the bitterness due to the resination of the wine is reduced. For those who want the aroma of the resin to dominate, resinated wines are best served at room temperature. Saltiness is increased by cold. Freezing will destroy cell tissue in certain plants as anyone who has tried to freeze a cucumber will know. This action will also make a dish with pepper in it taste more peppery after freezing.

While coldness may inhibit taste, heat enhances it by releasing aromatic oils in herbs and spices. This is a change in flavour which means that a vegetable which is quickly fried will not taste the same as one which has been slowly boiled. This holds good for a vegetable which is first fried and later stewed. The cook can exploit these situations to produce the required result.

Fresh herbs taste different to dried. Some, like bay leaf, are better used in dry form when some of the bitterness has left the leaf and the characteristic taste of laurel is more pronounced. Herbs and spices need careful storage. Herbs hung up to dry should not be allowed to get damp or they will go mouldy. In some homes dust may be a problem. Spices are best stored whole whenever possible and kept in airtight jars. The idea is to grind or grate when required.

The art of creating flavour is difficult to measure and is usually a matter of personal preference. Eye, taste, feeling and experience should be your guide to measurement. The quantities mentioned in the recipes, therefore, should serve only as a guide to your own experiments.

Much of Greece is mountainous and most of the country is not far from the sea. These conditions have provided the environment for a rich variety of herbs which the Greeks like to use in their cooking. The dill, parsley, savory, bay, thyme, mint, marjoram, cumin and coriander of the ancients have been supplemented by the tastes of the invaders. Basil, which the Greeks love with tomato dishes, was brought by the Venetians. With the development of the spice trade, allspice, cloves, cinnamon and nutmeg have found a place both in sweet and savoury cooking.

ALLSPICE (*bahári*): A member of the myrtle family, *Pimenta dioica* or *P. officinalis* is native to the West Indies, Central and South America. The island of Jamaica produces most of the world's supply. The tree has purple, myrtle-like berries which are picked while still green and dried in the sun. They turn brown and look like large peppercorns. Known in France and Spain as Jamaican pepper, allspice tastes like a mixture of cloves, cinnamon and nutmeg (hence the name). It should be stored whole.

ANISE or SWEET CUMIN (*glikánison*): *Pimpinella anisum* is a member of the parsley family and is thought to be the oldest-known spice, used by the ancient Egyptians, Greeks and Romans. The small pale seed contains the essential oil anethole which is used medicinally and for flavouring. The characteristic aniseed taste occurs in the drinks of most of the countries around the Mediterranean, though it is less popular in Italy. It is used as the flavouring in ouzo and sometimes in raki (arrak).

Add ouzo to dried figs and chestnuts. Put it in fig cake and in vegetable balls.

Infusions of anise are used in gastric and intestinal disorders, digestive spasms, to stimulate appetite (hence the apéritif ouzo), to relieve flatulence and coughing, and to stimulate mammary secretion.

BASIL (*vassíliko*): *Ocimum basilicum* is a member of the mint family and is named after the Greek patriarch Saint Basil (*c.* AD 329–379) whose feast day is 14 June. This green-leaved herb can be used wherever there are tomatoes. Use it with garlic in pasta sauces. It also goes well with green peppers, aubergines and eggs. Basil vinegar, made by macerating basil leaves in wine vinegar, makes a nice herb vinegar for use in the winter months. For a quick Greek snack cut a nice thick slice of wholewheat bread and put some slices of tomato on it. Sprinkle with salt, olive oil and fresh basil leaves and munch with a glass of red wine. The basil leaf should be broken up with the hands rather than chopped. Add some olives and cheese and you have a feast!

BAY or SWEET LAUREL (*dháfni*): A crown made from the leaves of *Laurus nobilis* was the symbol of wisdom in ancient Greece and was worn by military and sporting champions alike. The plant was sacred to the god Apollo and the name 'Daphne' still occurs in Greece today. Strongly scented and bitter when fresh, some cooks prefer the dried leaves, but old dry leaves with little or no taste should be discarded. The leaves are used to flavour dishes and are also used in pickling olives and in the packaging of figs.

BORAGE (*borándza* or *vúglosson*): *Borago officinalis* is indigenous to the Mediterranean but is now common on chalky soils in Europe. Its flowers are a bright sky blue and it smells something like a cucumber, having a pleasant, pungent taste. It is gathered wild in Greece, especially in Crete, and is collected for medicinal purposes (as *Herba boraginis*) at the beginning of the flowering period. Borage was known in ancient times as an aphrodisiac. An infusion was also said to be a good cure for hangovers.

Use the young leaves and flowers in salads. The hairy leaves may also be used, but should be finely chopped. Like cucumber, borage is delicious with yogurt or a cream cheese. Use it also as a stuffing for pasta, with aubergines or courgettes. When boiled it can be used like spinach. Borage is a main ingredient in mountain herb salads made in the villages.

Relatives of borage which can be found in Europe are comfrey (*Symphytum officinale*) and viper's bugloss (*Echium vulgare*) which may be used in similar ways in cooking.

CAMOMILE (*hamomíli*): *Anthemis nobilis* is an aromatic plant of the daisy family. Its daisy-like flowers are used medicinally and to make a tea for inducing sound sleep. The Greek name refers to the apple-like scent of the flowers. In Greece this daisy appears in spring and is dried in the sun before being stored in airtight jars. In the winter it is used to make infusions against chills, colds and stomach upsets. Doctors also prescribe the tea for making compresses and eye baths.

CINNAMON (*kanélla*): *Cinnamomum zeylanicum* was brought to Greece from Asia. It can be recognized by its pale brown tubes of thin tree bark and it is more delicate both in appearance and flavour than the dried inner bark of cassia (*Cinnamomum cassia*) which is frequently sold as cinnamon. Cinnamon is a digestive and is used in both sweet and savoury cooking. It is credited with reducing fever and in alleviating stomach disorders.

CLOVES (*garífalo* or *baharikó*): The dried fruit of a tree now known as *Eugenia aromatica* which became the basis of the spice trade. Cloves found their way into Greek cookery through trade with merchants from Southeast Asia and China. In Greece the clove pink or clove carnation often goes by the same name due to its beautiful clove-like scent.

CORIANDER (*maidanó*): *Coriandrum sativum* is perhaps the most commonly used flavouring herb in the world. The ancient Greeks introduced it to the Romans who brought it to England where it was used in English cooking up to Elizabethan times. In classical cookery, coriander seed is almost always used in dishes which are *à la greque*. Green coriander leaves are used in salads and with fresh tomatoes, chopped with small amounts of fresh onion. Greeks often call these green leaves parsley (*maidanó*) and in many places it is this herb that is grown and preferred. Wherever the recipes call for parsley, coriander leaves may be used if you prefer the taste.

CUMIN (*kímino*): *Cuminum cyminum* is indigenous to Greece and, like basil, some cooks do not use it. This delicate member of the parsley family grows to about 1 foot (30 cm) with mauve and white flowers. Originally from the East, it has been grown in the Mediterranean region for over 2000 years and was used by the Romans as a form of pepper. Its seeds should not be confused with the darker and thinner caraway seed which is used in bread and cakes. Cumin is well known for its medicinal properties and it is used, along with fennel or aniseed, to make gripe water for babies.

DANDELION (*radhíki* or *agrioradhíki*); *Taraxacum officinale* is valuable in winter as a salad plant and it can be cooked like spinach. The leaves should be young and torn up rather than chopped. Dandelion has a strong action on the kidneys and is a blood cleanser. As well as being beneficial to the kidneys it is an aid to digestion and the action of the liver and gall bladder.

Of all tastes, bitterness can be detected in the smallest quantity. This element of taste in the dandelion can be reduced by boiling and discarding the water. Bitterness cannot be counteracted by other flavours in the same way as sourness. It increases the effect of sourness and is more pronounced in cold dishes. These factors need to be remembered when preparing dandelion salad.

DILL (*ânitho*): *Anethum graveolens* is an important herb of the parsley family which was used by the ancient Greeks and Romans. The bitter flavour of the seed is quite different to the taste of the leaf due to the presence of carvone, the same essential oil which is found in caraway seed. Greek greengrocers sell it in bundles to use with spring onions, parsley and celery tops. The leaves should always be used fresh. They are excellent with potatoes, white cheese and salads and in white sauce, soups and omelettes.

FENNEL (*máratho*): The green herb *Foeniculum vulgare*, another member of the parsley family, was used in medicine long before it was used in cookery. Fennel seeds taste strongly of anise, containing large quantities of the essential oil anethole. It is an ingredient in gripe water for babies and is a good digestive and breath sweetener.

GARLIC (*skórdho*): The firm white bulbs of *Allium sativum*, a member of the lily family, have been known as essential to good health since ancient times. Homer recounts how Ulysses escaped from the enchantress Circe by the use or garlic as if to emphasize the marvellous attributes of this plant. Garlic contains antiseptic compounds which tone up the digestive system, reduce blood pressure and clear bronchitis.

Raw garlic has both flavour and pungency and is an essential ingredient in *skordhália*, a potato salad with garlic. Where the recipes call for its use it should not be omitted unless the taste is actually disliked.

MARJORAM or ORIGANUM (*rígani*): This member of the mint family is not the herb in Italian cookery known as oregano (*Origanum vulgare*); neither is it the wild marjoram of the English chalk downs. In Greece some ten different species grow wild on the mountain slopes and are known as *rígani*. It is probably the most widely used herb in Greek cookery. The most common varieties on sale are *O. hortensis*, *O. heraclesticum*, *O. smyrnaicum* and *O. paniflorum*. The flower heads tend to be purple, growing in thick clusters which distinguish them from the more pinkish wild marjoram (*O. vulgare*). Fresh marjoram has a marvellously pungent flavour and if you have access to it do not hesitate to sample some. On Crete, a plant known as *dhíktamo* or *maliarahórta* (hairy herb), the Cretan dittany, is also used as a food flavouring, but the plant is mainly used for medicinal purposes. This particular *rígani* is *O. dictamnus*.

If you cannot get *rígani*, use oregano which is nearer in flavour than wild marjoram.

MINT (*dhiósmo*): There are many mint species and hybrids common to the Mediterranean and Western Asia, tending to vary according to soil and climate. Among the best for culinary purposes are the varieties of *Mentha rotundifolia,* the round-leaved mint. Another common mint, probably brought to Britain by the Romans, is varieties of spearmint (*M. spicata*).

The ancient Greeks associated the aroma of mint with strength and warriors rubbed their bodies with it. Since it does not blend easily with other herbs, mint is best used on its own. It is excellent with potatoes, peas and beans, lentils, cucumber, tomatoes, aubergines and mushrooms. The flavour of dried mint is inferior to fresh.

MUSTARD (*mustárdha*): White mustard (*Sinapis alba* or *Brassica hirta*) is native to the Mediterranean. It was used by the ancient Greeks and the Romans who brought it to Britain. It must be allowed to mix with cold water before use so that the bitter glucoside in the seed can react with the water to produce the pungent taste. If this process is inhibited too early, by hot water or vinegar for example, a bitter taste will remain. Mustard goes very well in certain salad dressings and in sauces for vegetables of its own family (the cabbage family).

MYRTLE (*mirtiá*): *Myrtus communis* is a bush with fragrant flowers and leaves which grows on the mountain slopes of the Mediterranean. Together with rosemary and thyme, it is one of the characteristic perfumes in the air of Mediterranean hillsides. The white flowers give way to dark aromatic purple berries in late summer. These berries were dried and used like pepper by the ancient Greeks.

The myrtle plant is popular among the shepherds and mountain people of Greece. Apart from the use of berries, soft cheeses are sometimes wrapped in the leaves which marks the cheese with a delicious and elusive fragrance.

NUTMEG (*moshokáridho*): The round or oval fruit of the tropical plant *Myristica fragrans*. The dark hard fruit is found encased in a basket-like structure which is known as mace when dry. It is best to grate nutmeg straight into a dish and not to buy powdered nutmeg which has lost much of its flavour. Nutmeg goes well with spinach and with cheese.

PARSLEY (*maidanó*): According to Homer, parsley (*Petroselinum crispum* or *P. hortense*) was fed to the chariot horses to give them extra vigour. Victors at the Greek games were often garlanded with parsley and it seems to have been used by the ancient Greeks and Romans for ceremonial purposes. Probably the most commonly used herb in Western cookery, it is widely used by the Greeks though many cooks prefer to use coriander leaf. The word *maidanó* is therefore used to describe both herbs in ordinary speech. Like parsley, coriander is in leaf all the year round in Greece.

ROSEMARY (*dhendhrolívano*): This member of the mint family (*Rosmarinus officinalis*) grows as a wild evergreen bush in the Mediterranean. It is very aromatic and its essential oil contains the easily recognizable camphor. It is one of the most common wild aromatic plants of Mediterranean hillsides, especially those on rocky limestone soils near the sea. The herb is most popular in the areas in Greece where there is an Italian influence in the cookery. It is good in soups made with peas or beans. Much of the flavour tends to be lost after drying.

SAGE (*faskómilo*): The ancient Greeks and Romans used sage in medicine and its botanical name *Salvia officinalis* comes from the Latin *salvere* – to save, because of its renowned properties in maintaining health. It has a strong aromatic flavour which, as in rosemary, is reminiscent of camphor. There are many varieties, all differing in strength and flavour. It may occur in village salads, but its most popular use in Greece is as a tea, especially in the mountainous regions. The infusion has the same name as the herb and the Cretans still prefer this instead of tea (see Sage Tea, p. 153).

SESAME (*susámi*): The small, pale brown seeds of *Sesamum indicum* were used by the ancient Greeks, Egyptians and Persians. The seeds produce an almost odourless oil which keeps well in hot countries. It is the main ingredient in the sweetmeat *halvás*, the making of which has become an industry centred on the northern city of Thessaloniki in Macedonia. The most well-known product of sesame is the paste known as *tahíni* which is made by grinding the seeds very finely. Tahini is used as a base for salad dressings and to flavour crushed chick peas in the dish *húmus*.

THYME (*thimári*): Another member of the mint family, *Thymus vulgaris* was used by the ancient Greeks to whom the aroma signified grace and courage because the herb was sacred to Aphrodite (Venus) and Ares (Mars). Thyme contains the essential oil thymol which is an antiseptic, disinfectant and preservative. The wild plant of the Greek mountains is small and bushy with grey-green leaves and purple flowers, and is not to be confused with marjoram.

It is good with tomatoes, potatoes, courgettes, aubergines and peppers. It blends well with wine, brandy, onion and garlic in casseroles. It is sometimes used to flavour olives in the pickling process.

Basic Ingredients –
The Stock Cupboard

This wholefood cookbook uses traditional Greek dishes as well as adapting some modern ones to create a Greek cuisine for the vegetarian. The Greek style should recommend itself to vegetarians and wholefood enthusiasts alike. The principles of the style are simple, locally produced food with freshly gathered herbs; meals that are frequently eaten communally with the accent on simplicity, goodness and nourishment rather than presentation and effect; meals eaten slowly with the minimum of fuss and the maximum of enjoyment. Thus, home-produced fare should come first, followed by organically grown food whenever possible and foods which are as unadulterated as you can obtain.

CHEESE (*tirí*): Traditionally, Greek cheeses are made from goat's or sheep's milk from recipes which have been handed down in the villages through the generations. For an authentic Greek flavour in your cookery use goat's milk products instead of cow's milk. The number of suppliers is increasing all the time and this will grow if the demand is there. Good goat's milk has a rich, creamy texture and is a little more tasty than cow's milk. The difference in taste is generally due to the richness and variety of the goat's diet. A comparison could be made with the battery hen and free-range hen. The use of goat's milk yogurt and local goat's cheese will bring your cookery closer to the Greek original.

Cheeses are produced in great variety though most of them are still unknown outside Greece. Cow's milk is imported into most areas and country people do not rely on it for cheese-making. If you cannot obtain the authentic Greek cheese, use the nearest equivalent which is suggested in the recipes. For details of cheese varieties see the chapter on Cheese, pp. 124–7.

CLARIFIED BUTTER (*mayirihó vútiro*): Since ancient times it has been a custom in Greece to use clarified butter in cooking. Where this is mentioned in a recipe, use clarified butter or margarine rather than olive oil since the flavour is quite different. In Greece clarified butter is being replaced by *fitíni*, a vegetable fat made of olive oil and flavoured with a small amount of sheep's milk butter. Margarine made exclusively from olive oil is available in Greece.

Clarified margarine, marketed in Europe under the term 'vegetable ghee', is particularly good. It can be purchased in Greek, Asian and Middle Eastern stores and in wholefood shops. If you cannot obtain any of these products use ordinary butter, unsalted if possible, rather than cooking fat.

FILLO PASTRY (*fíllo*): This extremely thin pastry is best left to the experts since it is very tricky to make and is widely available in convenient packs. The pastry gets its name from the Greek word for leaf, which gives a good idea of its relative thickness. Puff pastry, though being the nearest substitute, will not give the best result.

To make *fíllo*, the pastry must be rolled out on a table and stretched on each side until it is paper thin. Later it is cut up into usable-sized pieces and it is these thin sheets which are put one on top of the other in Greek baking. The sheets can be bought in 400 g or 500 g packs, sometimes called 'strudel pastry'. Keep the pack refrigerated and wrapped in polythene or cling film. Although the sheets of fillo pastry are very thin, they are quite strong and easy to use. Pittas Pastries Ltd, 24 Old Farm Avenue, Southgate, London N14, are helpful if you have any difficulty in obtaining it.

FLOUR (*alévri*): Unless otherwise stated, use wholewheat flour. Greek village cooks use this and remove the bran with a sieve if a whiter flour is required. Always add enough liquid to make your doughs soft and pliable and knead them well to encourage this.

HONEY (*méli*): Honeys available in Greece are deliciously aromatic, the flavour depending on the herbs which the bees have been visiting. These will be predominantly rosemary, sage, origanum, thyme, or a mixture of wild herbs and flowers. Since so many of the flowering plants are mountain-lovers, you may see beehives, painted in shades of pale blue or green, balanced high up among the rocks as you travel around. Some honeys have a resinous quality derived from a nearby pine forest. Others may be scented with orange, lemon, eucalyptus or olive blossom. Remember that the delicate flavour of the honey you use will be driven off in cooking and that the sugars will caramelize.

LEMONS (*lemónia*): Although citrus fruits are thought to have originated in Southeast Asia, the lemon was cultivated in Greece by the end of the third century BC and is now thought of as a typical Mediterranean fruit. Indeed, it is difficult to imagine Greek cookery without this essential sun-coloured fruit. Lemons grow on small spiny trees which have white and purple blossom. The pale green leaves have a characteristically bitter taste. They are picked during Holy Week to symbolize the bitter passion of Christ.

The juice is a powerful souring agent, due to the presence of citric acid, though it is not as strong as wine vinegar. The aroma of lemon, present in the skin, is the essential lemon oil. Fresh lemon juice is always preferable to the packaged item.

OLIVES (*eliés*): A native of the Mediterranean, the olive is one of the oldest-known fruits, cultivated in Greece since prehistoric times. It was the ancient symbol of prosperity and fruitfulness and a crown of olive leaves was used for military and athletic victors and for wedding couples. The olive branch is still a symbol of peace. In legend, Athena the virgin goddess was made guardian of the great Greek city because she caused the first olive tree to grow. According to the Greek historian Herodotus (*c.* 485–425 BC), Athens was the centre of the Greek olive industry.

The evergreen tree, with its metallic green leaves, is an essential part of the Greek landscape and has been the mainstay of traditional rural economy. The fruit, preserved in brine and its own oil, along with bread and goat's milk, is an important part of the diet of village people, especially those living in remote mountainous regions. The crushed fruit gives an oil which is both a food and a cooking medium of exceptional nutritive value. The pulp may be dried and burned as a cheap source of fuel or it may be used as fertilizer or winter fodder. Olive tree foliage may be used as bedding for goats and sheep and the wood is an excellent material for making cooking utensils and containers. Greeks consider it fortunate that the Venetian invaders had the foresight to plant olive trees wherever they went. This legacy has left a profusion of olive groves in many parts of Greece. The island of Corfu, for example, is believed to have as many as four million olive trees.

The green berries turn black or red as they ripen. There are many varieties, differing in size, colour, oil and flavour. Size and appearance may have little bearing on flavour since many quite small olives of fine quality are to be found growing in remote mountain valleys. For this reason you should always taste before buying. Many parts of Greece produce an especially good olive. The port of Kalamata, for example, on the south coast of the Peloponnese to the west of Taiyetos, gives its name to the famed *Kalamáta* olives.

OLIVE OIL (*ládhi eliás* or *eleoládho*): The olive harvest (*eleomaémata*) comes at the end of autumn when the priest is often called to bless the olive trees and the presses which will be used to extract the oil. Every village has its olive press. The olives which have been sorted for making oil are ground between two large stones, usually turned by a mule or donkey, like the old British cider press. The whole of the olive is mashed to pulp which is put in large pieces of cloth and pressed in a wooden press. The golden green oil is collected in copper basins or in underground stone tanks to settle.

This is the moment of the first press and this oil, known as 'virgin' (*parthénon*) or 'extra virgin', is the very best for culinary purposes. Later presses produce a yellower or more pale oil which is more suitable for other uses such as lubrication, rubbing on the body, etc. Care should be taken in choosing oil for cooking. Put a little in the palm of the hand and rub the hands together. Now sniff the aroma. If it is not delicate and pleasant, the chances are that you will not enjoy it in your cooking.

Often a simple celebratory meal will take place after the first press. Fresh or toasted bread is drenched with some of the fresh oil. This is relished with a glass of wine and perhaps some nuts or dried figs. Hot fresh bread with newly pressed oil is one of the many simple wonders of rural Greek life. Taken with home-produced wine in the presence of smiling faces and appreciative exclamations, it is a gastronomic experience never to be forgotten.

PULSES (*óspria*): Another mainstay of rural life and a delight for the vegetarian are the dried legumes of Greece. Rich in protein and easily stored, pulses keep the villagers through the winter months and are the main ingredients in Lenten food.

The problem of flatulence, from which many lovers of pulses suffer, needs to be and can be overcome. The solution is frequent soaking. Chick peas, for example, should be soaked for two or three days before cooking. Wash the pulses well in cold water and pour off the water. Put in fresh water and leave them to soak. At night change the water and again the next morning. Continue this routine up to the time of cooking.

If you are in Greece in May, try to sample the young chick peas before they are dried. These are delicious with some olives and broad beans with a glass of ouzo.

RICE (*rízi*): Greeks like sweet and savoury rice dishes. The rice used in this book is long-grain brown rice which is now available in good supermarkets as well as wholefood stores.

SESAME PASTE (*tahíni*): The highly nutritious greyish paste of crushed sesame seeds. It can be bought in jars and should be well stirred before use to blend in any sesame oil which might have risen to the surface.

SUGAR (*záhari*): Since most people are seeking to cut down the amount of sugar in their diet, only a few recipes using sugar are included in this book. Use brown unrefined or good demerara sugar rather than white. Honey may be used where the dish will not be dominated by the strong flavour of the honey.

VINEGAR (*ksídhi*): The vinegar used in the recipes is always good wine vinegar which can be white or red. Do not substitute with brown malt vinegar which has a different taste. Wine vinegar is superior to lemon juice or malt vinegar as a dressing for salads and seems to cause less digestive upsets.

YOGURT (*yaúrti*): Another wonder of Greek rural life – sheep's milk yogurt! Considered by some to be the most exquisite of all yogurts, this is thick, rich and creamy and comes in earthenware bowls with a delicious crust on the top. Such a yogurt bears little resemblance to the sour watery product on sale throughout most of Europe. All the recipes use natural unflavoured yogurt.

Weights and Measures

It would be against the principles of Greek cookery to insist on exact measurements, though they are more critical in the baking recipes. Simple weights and measures are provided, in imperial and metric systems, as a starting point for your own experimentation. These may be varied according to taste and necessity.

The cup measure used in this book is one which holds 8 fluid ounces (225 ml) water, 6 ounces (170 g) rice, 4 ounces (100 g) flour.

The teaspoon holds approximately ⅙ fluid ounce (5 ml) and the tablespoon holds approximately ½ fluid ounce (15 ml).

Cup measurements are level. The spoon measurements are as much as the spoon will hold without being heaped. Cup and spoon sizes vary, but you will soon find the amounts which give the result you like best.

The recipes are sufficient for four to six people, unless otherwise stated.

Appetizers (*Orektiká*)

Appetizers may be served before the meal with drinks and apéritifs or they may accompany the meal as tasty little titbits. A great variety of these feature in the Greek cuisine and many of them are excellent to take on picnics. *Mezédhes* or *mezedhákia*, which are snacks and titbits to accompany a drink at any time of day or night, may not always be appetizers. The word *mezé* tends to be interchangeable with *orektikó*, but a series of *mezédhes* can make a meal in itself. This is often the meaning of the term when used on menus.

Young girls used to celebrate May Day by getting up early and going to the fields with a picnic basket to catch the magic of May – a custom dating back to ancient times. They would pick flowers to make wreaths and necklaces which were hung on the front doors when they came home to bring the magic and good luck of May to the house. Spring is the season of picnics and outings, when the days are not too hot. Picnics are made up with perhaps cheese triangles, vegetable balls, olives, cheeses, stuffed vine leaves, bread and wine.

Savoury Rolls (*Burekákia*)

Pasties of different sorts can be made with fillo pastry and rolled into cigar shapes or little envelopes.

1 cup cooked chick peas *or* cooked
  dried beans
1 tablespoon finely chopped onion
1 teaspoon chopped *or* dried herbs
pinch of nutmeg

pinch of salt
pinch of freshly ground pepper
clarified butter *or* olive oil
1 pack fillo pastry

Mash the chick peas and combine with the onion, herbs, and seasoning. Fry the filling mixture in a tablespoon of butter for 5 minutes. Put a sheet of fillo on the pastry board and cut it into two pieces, making sheets about 6 × 8 inches (15 × 20 cm). Melt some butter and keep it handy. Brush one of the pieces of fillo with butter. Spread a teaspoon of filling along one end and roll over once. Turn in the edges of the pastry and roll up to make a cigar shape. When the filling or pastry is used up put the burekakia on greased baking trays and bake in a moderate oven until golden (about 15 minutes). Wrap any leftover pastry in clingfilm and keep in the refrigerator.

    Burekakia can be deep-fried in olive oil or butter, in which case there is no need to brush the pastry with butter. If you do not want the filling to be fried, beat in an egg and a tablespoon or two of wine. Mix well and use as your filling. Mashed vegetables, potato, nuts and chestnuts all make good fillings as long as the mixture is kept fairly dry.

Spinach Pasties (*Spanakópitakia*)

1 lb (450 g) spinach
2 spring onions
2 oz (50 g) feta cheese

1 teaspoon chopped dill leaf *or*
  coriander leaf
clarified butter *or* olive oil
1 pack fillo pastry

Chop the spinach and onions and boil together in a little water until the spinach is soft. Mash. Mash the cheese and beat it into the spinach with the chopped herb. Melt a little butter and keep it handy. Put a sheet of fillo on the pastry board and cut it in two pieces, making sheets about 8 × 12 inches (20 × 30 cm). Brush one of the pieces of fillo with butter and fold it in half. Brush again with butter. Put some filling at one end and fold up to make an envelope. Put the pasties on greased baking sheets and bake in a moderate oven until golden (15–25 minutes). Wrap any leftover pastry in clingfilm and keep in the refrigerator.

Cheese Pasties (*Tirópatakia*)

½ lb (225 g) feta cheese
1–2 eggs, beaten
2 teaspoons finely chopped parsley
  or coriander leaf

pinch of freshly ground pepper
clarified butter *or* olive oil
1 pack fillo pastry

Mash the cheese with a fork in a bowl. Beat in the eggs, herbs and seasoning. Melt some butter and keep it handy. Put a sheet of fillo on the pastry board and cut it in half. Brush with melted butter. Fold the sheet in half and brush with butter again. Put a little of the filling at one end and fold up to make an envelope. Put the pasties on greased baking trays and bake in a moderate oven until golden (15–25 minutes).

Other cheese mixtures could be used in this recipe. Use other herbs and add ingredients like chopped nuts. Tangy herbs like sage or rosemary, for example, are excellent with curd cheeses.

Potato Balls (*Patátes Keftédhes*)

1 lb (450 g) potatoes
½ teaspoon salt
4 spring onions, finely chopped
1 cup cooked cauliflower florets *or*
  peas

1 tablespoon chopped fresh mint
  leaves
juice of ½ lemon
flour
olive oil for frying

Boil the potatoes in salted water until they are soft. Peel and mash. Mix in the onion, cauliflower, mint leaf and lemon juice. Beat well to make a smooth mixture. Divide into walnut-sized balls and roll in flour on a pastry board. Fry in hot olive oil until golden.

Serve hot or cold. Potato balls are excellent for picnic fare or with a salad.

Spinach Balls (*Spanakókeftedhes*)

1 lb (450 g) spinach
2–4 cloves garlic, finely chopped
½ teaspoon salt
½ cup feta cheese

½ teaspoon ground aniseed
flour
olive oil

Cook the spinach in boiling water for 5 minutes. Rinse well and drain. Mash the spinach or purée in a liquidizer. Add the garlic, salt, cheese and aniseed and mix well. Add enough flour to make a stiff mixture. Divide the mixture into walnut-sized balls and fry in hot olive oil until golden. Serve hot or cold.

Squash Balls (*Kolokíthi Keftédhes*)

A typical autumn sight in some Greek villages is the rich orange globes of drying pumpkins ripening on the flat roofs of whitewashed houses. Interestingly, the English word for pumpkin comes via the ancient Greek for 'ripe' (*pepón*).

1 lb (450 g) pumpkin, marrow *or* other squash
1 small onion, finely chopped
½ teaspoon chopped sage leaf

1 tablespoon finely chopped parsley *or* coriander leaf
½ teaspoon salt
flour
olive oil for frying

Peel the pumpkin and cut into cubes. Boil in the minimum of water until just soft. Mash with the onion, herbs and salt. Add enough flour to make a stiff mixture and roll into walnut-sized balls. Fry in hot olive oil until golden. Serve hot or cold.

Like all vegetable balls, these are very good in a picnic or with a salad.

Stuffed Vine Leaves (*Dholmádhes*)

Pickled vine leaves are available loose or in polythene packets. Rinse them and allow to blanch in boiling water for 2–3 minutes. Rinse again. Fresh vine leaves need to be boiled in the same way. Strain and rinse in cold water. Like all stuffed dishes, there is endless scope to create different mixtures. Here is a recipe using rice and beans:

2 tablespoons olive oil
1 onion, finely chopped
1 cup cooked beans, mashed
½ cup rice
2 tablespoons finely chopped walnuts *or* pine nuts
2 tablespoons tomato paste

2 tablespoons chopped dill leaf *or* parsley
1 teaspoon salt
pinch of freshly ground pepper
40–50 vine leaves
lemon juice

Heat the oil in a pan and gently fry the onion until it becomes transparent. Add the beans, rice, nuts, tomato paste and herbs. Sprinkle with salt and pepper and mix well. Add half a cup of water and cook gently until the water is absorbed. Allow to cool. Put a vine leaf face downwards (vein side up) on a chopping board. Remove any stalk. Put a small amount of stuffing mixture in the centre and fold it up like an envelope. First fold in the base of the leaf, then the two sides, finally roll it up with the tip tucked underneath. Do not wrap the leaves too tightly since the rice will expand during the next stage of the cooking. Put the packets side by side in a heavy pan in layers. Add water until it is just below the top of the dholmadhes. Put a plate or a saucer on the top of them and press gently. This small weight will keep the little packets together during the cooking. Put the lid on the pan and cook on a gentle heat for half an hour. Check from time to time to make sure the water does not dry up. Test after 30 minutes to see if the rice is tender. If not carry on gently cooking. Remove the dholmadhes and allow to cool. Sprinkle with lemon juice before serving.

Dholmadhes may also be served with a sauce (see Sauces, pp. 128–32) or some fresh natural yogurt. They are excellent with an apéritif. Other ingredients which could be included in a stuffing are chopped dried apricots, sultanas, garlic, fresh tomato. Use different herbs which will blend well with the delicious lemon taste of the vine leaves. For use as a mezé, make the dholmadhes as small as possible.

Assuming that most people will be able to eat 4 or 5 dholmadhes, the recipe is enough for 10 or 12 people.

Stuffed Eggs (Avgá Yemistá)

4 eggs
1 small onion, finely chopped
2 cloves garlic, finely chopped
2 tablespoons chopped parsley or coriander leaf
1 teaspoon salt
pinch of freshly ground pepper
1 tablespoon yogurt
1 tablespoon olive oil
1 lemon

Boil the eggs until they are hard (6–10 minutes). Allow to cool. Shell and slice in half. Remove the yolks. Mash the yolks with the onion and garlic. Stir in the herbs, seasoning and yogurt. Gradually stir in the oil until the mixture is well blended. Arrange the egg whites on a dish and spoon in the stuffing mixture. Serve with slices of lemon.

Aubergine Dip (Melitzánosaláta)

2 large aubergines
1 small onion, finely chopped
2 cloves garlic, finely chopped
1 teaspoon salt
pinch of freshly ground pepper
3 tablespoons olive oil
juice of ½ lemon or 3 tablespoons wine vinegar
1 tablespoon chopped parsley or coriander leaf

Heat the aubergines under the grill so that they brown all over and begin to crack. They may be heated in a similar way in a heavy frying pan. Leave to cool and prepare the rest of the ingredients. Take the skin off the aubergines and beat the flesh with a fork. Beat in the onion, garlic, salt and pepper. Gradually add the olive oil to make a stiff paste. Beat in the lemon juice and serve cold garnished with green herbs.

Serve as a dip with pieces of fresh or toasted bread or pitta bread. The dip may also be served already spread on pieces of bread. Small pieces of fresh tomato and green pepper could be beaten into the dip to give extra taste and colour. For a nice cheese taste add ½ cup of crumbled feta cheese and substitute a sliced spring onion or a tablespoon of chopped chives for the chopped onion.

Aubergine and Sesame Dip
(*Melitzánosaláta ke Tahíni*)

1 large aubergine
1 teaspoon salt
pinch of freshly ground pepper
½ cup sesame paste
juice of 1 lemon

1–2 cloves garlic, finely chopped
3 tablespoons olive oil
1 tablespoon chopped parsely *or* coriander leaf

Char the aubergine until the skin cracks as in the previous recipe. Remove the skin. Mash the flesh with a fork and sprinkle with salt and pepper. Put the sesame paste in a bowl and stir in the lemon juice and garlic. Gradually stir in the oil and mix in the aubergine. Serve sprinkled with green herb. The dish could be decorated with slices of lemon.

Chestnut Dip (*Kástanosalata*)

2 cups cooked chestnuts
1 tablespoon finely chopped onion
2 tablespoons finely chopped celery
1 cup yogurt

1 teaspoon salt
freshly ground pepper to taste
1 tablespoon chopped parsley *or* coriander leaf

Mash the chestnuts and mix in the onion, celery, yogurt and seasoning. Serve sprinkled with chopped herbs.

Chick Pea and Sesame Dip (*Húmus*)

1 cup cooked chick peas
2 tablespoons sesame paste
4 tablespoons olive oil
2 cloves garlic, finely chopped

juice of ½ lemon
salt
½ lemon, cut in slices
black olives

Mash the chick peas in a bowl. Stir in the sesame paste, oil, garlic, lemon juice and salt to taste. Mix together to form a thick sauce, adding a little water if necessary. Taste the sauce and add any of the above ingredients according to your taste. Garnish with lemon slices and olives. Serve cold with bread, celery and cucumber.

Other garnishes could include chopped green herbs or finely sliced onion.

Chick Pea and Yogurt Dip (*Revíthi ke Yaúrtisaláta*)

1 cup cooked chick peas
4 tablespoons yogurt
2 cloves garlic, finely chopped
4 tablespoons olive oil
4 tablespoons lemon juice

salt
freshly ground pepper
1 tablespoon chopped parsley *or* coriander leaf

Mash the chick peas in a bowl and mix in the yogurt, garlic, oil and lemon juice. Season with salt and pepper to taste and garnish with chopped herbs. Serve with bread and olives.

Cucumber and Yogurt Dip (*Dzadzíki*)

1 cup finely diced cucumber (grating will make the cucumber watery)
1 cup yogurt
1 clove garlic, finely chopped
4 tablespoons olive oil

salt
freshly ground pepper
2 teaspoons chopped mint leaf
1 tablespoon chopped parsley *or* coriander leaf

Mix the cucumber with the yogurt in a bowl. Stir in the garlic, oil, salt and pepper to taste and mint. Blend well and serve chilled with a garnish of chopped herbs.

This is one of the classic Greek dips.

Garlic Sauce with Walnut Dip (*Skordhália me Karídhi*)

3 slices bread
4 cloves garlic
1 cup walnuts *or* blanched almonds

½ teaspoon salt
1 cup olive oil
1 tablespoon wine vinegar

Soak the bread in a little warm water for a few minutes and squeeze out to make a pulp. Grind the garlic with the nuts, salt and a tablespoon of oil. Mix well with the bread pulp. Stir in the vinegar. Add the rest of the oil by gradually stirring it in to make a thick sauce. Serve cold with bread, celery sticks and cucumber.

Sesame Dip (*Tahíni*)

2 cloves garlic
juice of 1 lemon
½ teaspoon salt
½ cup sesame paste

1 tablespoon finely chopped
   parsley *or* coriander leaf
½ teaspoon sesame seeds, lightly
   toasted

Grind the garlic with the lemon juice and salt. Mix in a bowl with the sesame paste to make a thick sauce, adding a little water if necessary. Garnish with the herbs and sesame seeds. Serve cold with bread, olives and slices of lemon.

Fresh Artichokes (*Angináres*)

This is the Cretan way to eat an artichoke as an appetizer or *mezé*. Each person will need 1 small artichoke, 1 lemon, some salt and a sharp knife. Pull off the spiny leaves until you reach the inside heart. Keep the leaves. Cut out the hairy part. You now have three parts of the artichoke head which can be eaten. The top of the stem can be sliced. Cut the heart into a few slices. Arrange the slices with any fleshy leaves on a plate. Sprinkle liberally with lemon juice and salt to taste. The fleshy base of the spiny leaves can be eaten along with the sliced heart and stalk. Serve with salted nuts and ouzo or raki.

Artichoke with Eggs (*Angináres me Avgá*)

Prepare the artichoke as in the previous recipe. Hard boil an egg for each artichoke. Mash the egg in a bowl with a fork and mix in lemon juice and olive oil to make a thick sauce. Sprinkle with salt. Either dip the artichoke pieces into the egg mixture or chop the artichoke finely and mix in with the egg to form a dip for bread.

Fried Cheese (*Saganáki*)

kefalotíri cheese
olive oil
lemon

marjoram *or* other dried herb
bread

Cut the cheese into small thick squares. Cover the bottom of a frying
pan (*saganáki*) with oil and fry the cheese slices on both sides until
golden. Sprinkle with lemon juice and a little dried herbs and serve
with slices of lemon and bread.

Some cooks dust the cheese in flour before frying. When any hard
cheese is cut in squares and fried in hot olive oil, or browned under the
grill, the pieces are known as *tirákia*.

Chestnut Patties (*Kastáno Keftédhes*)

2 cups cooked chestnuts
1 small onion, finely chopped
1 tablespoon finely chopped
   parsley *or* coriander leaf
½ teaspoon crumbled sage
1 tablespoon crumbled feta cheese

1 teaspoon cumin powder
salt
freshly ground pepper
2 eggs, well beaten
flour
olive oil for frying

Mash the chestnuts in a bowl and mix in the rest of the ingredients
except the flour and oil, with the seasoning to taste. Make the mixture
up into walnut-sized balls with the help of a little flour. Fry in hot oil
until golden. Serve hot or cold.

Bread (*Psomí*)

The young green wheat appears in the fields at springtime. Spring begins officially in Greece on 1 March. In former times the guardian of the village (*skopós*) would announce the coming of spring by blowing on a conch shell. When the new wheat appears, the fields display the promise of a continuing supply of flour for breadmaking. On saints' days and other special occasions, when the priest is called to bless the bread that is passed around, slightly sweet bread is usually used, known as holy bread (*áyos ártos*). In some villages a very hard bread is baked (*paksimádhia*) which must be soaked in water before it can be eaten. Its consistency is very much like a baby's rusk.

Notes on Breadmaking

All the bread recipes use 100 per cent wholewheat flour unless another type of flour is stated. In Greek villages the bread is made whiter by sieving out the bran. If your diet has very little roughage in it then the bran is best left in. A few precautions will ensure success with your bread:

Warm utensils are better than cold. If you turn on the oven before you start, you can use the heat from it to keep things warm. This is what makes breadmaking so attractive in the winter months! If there is room in the oven, something else could be baked or cooked at the same time, for example a casserole. Allow the yeast to ferment with sugar and *warm* water. It will double its volume in 10 minutes. If it does not froth up, the yeast is dead and cannot be used. Do not add boiling water to yeast.

Add enough warm water to make a smooth dough. Knead well until the dough is nice and pliable. Kneading is an important part of breadmaking and should not be skimped. A simple method of kneading is to fold the dough in half and press down on it with the clenched fist or heel of the hand, allowing your weight to bear down from the shoulder rather than the wrist. Knead generously, repeating this operation. Keep the dough in a draught-free place and allow it to double its size. Knead the dough again.

When bread is cooked it has a hollow sound when tapped underneath. Allow bread to cool before storing.

Toast (*Friganiá*)

Greeks like to eat bread when it is warm or gently toasted. It is not usually browned. Thick slices of bread are lightly toasted so that they just have a crisp texture on the outside. Lightly toasted bread is excellent with dips and sauces. Some Greeks start the day with a little toasted bread dipped in olive oil and a glass of wine.

Country Bread (*Horiátiko Psomí*)

In some Greek villages people still take their baking to be done in the baker's oven. If you want to know where the baker's is when you need some bread in a strange village ask for the oven (*fúrno*). The baker's oven is particularly useful during festival time when large amounts of baking need to be done.

2 tablespoons sugar
1 tablespoon dried yeast
1 cup milk

2 tablespoons margarine *or* clarified
   butter
1 teaspoon salt
4½ cups flour

Put a tablespoon of sugar in a jug and sprinkle with yeast. Add ½ cup of warm water and allow the yeast mixture to double its size in a warm place (about 10 minutes). Heat the milk gently in a saucepan and stir in the rest of the sugar, margarine and salt. Sift the flour into a mixing bowl. Make a well in the middle and pour in the yeast mixture. Stir in with a large knife. Stir in the warm milk mixture. Clean the knife and knead the dough well with the hands. Allow it to double its size in a warm place (1–1½ hours). Knead the dough again and allow it to rise for a further 1–1½ hours. Knead again for a few minutes and break into two loaves. Put each loaf in a greased baking tin or leave round on a greased baking tray. Brush the tops of the loaves with melted butter or margarine and cover with a cloth. Allow the loaves to rise again for a further hour. While they are doing this, turn on the oven to 375°F/190°C/Gas 5. When the loaves have risen bake them in the oven until they are golden (about 45 minutes).

Pitta Bread (*Pítta*)

Traditionally this oval, flat bread was baked on the convex side of an iron saucer-shaped skillet over a wood fire or on the outside of a clay oven. It can now be bought in Greek, Asian and Middle Eastern stores. Like many other Greek words, pitta has passed into the English language.

¾ tablespoon dried yeast   1–2 teaspoons salt
1 tablespoon sugar   1 tablespoon olive oil
4 cups flour

Turn on the oven to 350°F/180°C/Gas 4. Put the mixing bowl and utensils on the top of the cooker to warm up. Mix the yeast with the sugar in a small jug and add a cup of warm water. Allow to stand for 10 minutes to ferment. Sift the flour with the salt in a mixing bowl and make a well in the middle. Pour in the yeast mixture and stir into the flour with a knife. Clean the knife and mix and knead the dough with the hands. Gradually add half a cup (more or less according to the flour used) of warm water and mix with the hands until a dough is formed which does not stick to the fingers or the sides of the bowl. Knead with the fists for 10 minutes until the dough is smooth and elastic. Add a drop more water if necessary. Now gradually add the oil to the dough, kneading it well. Cover the bowl with a cloth and leave on the top of the cooker to double its size. In a warm place this will only take an hour. Knead the dough again for 2–3 minutes until it is quite smooth. Break the dough into 6 equal pieces. Roll out each piece on a floured pastry board and pull out to make a flattened oval shape. Roll out until the dough is about ¼ inch (6 mm) thick. Put 2 pittas on a greased baking sheet and bake in the oven until they just begin to turn golden (25–30 minutes). Do not allow them to become hard. As soon as a fork can slip in and out of them easily they are done. Wrap the cooked pittas in a cloth and put on a wire rack to cool. Store in a plastic bag in the refrigerator.

Pittas can be used immediately. Make a slit in the side and fill with a salad or other filling or cut in half and butter. When using pittas from store, allow them to heat gently under the grill or in the oven for a few minutes before cutting them open.

If you want to make Greek village pittas, make your dough pieces into a ball and roll out a round shape. Bake in the oven or in an iron frying pan by baking on both sides over a low heat. Makes 6 good-sized pittas.

Wraparound Pitta (*Yíropitta*)

Greece is moving into the era of the instant meal with the stuffed pitta and the wraparound pitta (*yíropitta*) which can be bought in cafés and wayside stalls. Make round pittas as in the previous recipe. These are then wrapped around a tasty filling.

For the filling:

chopped tomato	finely chopped coriander leaf
chopped cucumber	yogurt
sliced onion	pinch of dried herbs
finely chopped garlic	salt and pepper to taste

Festival Bread (*Tsuréki*)

Tsureki is a sweet, plaited brioche eaten during the Easter and Christmas festivals. It is delicious in the morning for breakfast or with coffee later in the day.

1 tablespoon dried yeast	3 eggs
¾ cup sugar	1 cup warm milk
4 oz (110 g) clarified butter *or* margarine	5½ cups flour

Turn on the oven to 275°F/140°C/Gas 1. Put your mixing bowl and utensils on the top of the oven to warm. Mix the yeast with a tablespoon of sugar in a jug. Add ½ cup warm water and allow the yeast to ferment for 10 minutes. Cream the butter and the rest of the sugar by beating together in a large mixing bowl until smooth. Beat in 2 eggs, one at a time, and mix well. Gradually add the warm milk. Add the yeast mixture. Blend in the flour, cup by cup, using a long knife until the dough becomes quite heavy. Clean the knife and continue kneading with the hands. Knead the dough for 10–15 minutes until it is smooth and pliable. Cover with a tea towel and leave in a draught-free place (on top of the cooker) to double its size (about 1 hour). Knead the dough again for 2–3 minutes until it is quite smooth. With floured hands, divide the dough into 6 equal pieces. Roll out each piece to make a thick rope about 18 inches (45 cm) long. Take three ropes, pinching them together at the end to join them. Plait the three ropes, pinch together and tuck the end underneath. Do this twice. Put the two loaves on greased baking sheets and cover with a cloth. If the dough tends to flatten put the loaves in bread tins to contain them. Turn up the oven to 350°F/180°C/Gas 4. Keep the loaves in the same draught-free place until they double their size. Beat the remaining egg and brush the top of each loaf to glaze. Bake in the oven until golden (30–40 minutes). Test each loaf with a fork which should come out cleanly.

At Eastertime place a dyed red Easter egg in the middle of the plaited dough before it is put aside to rise again (see Easter Eggs, p. 121). Allow to bake along with the loaf. If you like the brioche to have a slightly scented flavour add 1–2 tablespoons of rosewater to the dough. Add a little more flour if necessary.

Spicy Easter Bread (*Lambrópsomo*)

2 teaspoons cloves	4 oz (110 g) clarified butter *or*
2 small pieces cinnamon	margarine
2 bay leaves	3 eggs
½ teaspoon grated nutmeg	1 cup warm milk
1 tablespoon yeast	6 cups flour
¾ cup sugar	2 tablespoons sesame seeds

Put all the spices in a small saucepan and add a cup of water. Simmer gently for 30 minutes; do not allow the liquid to dry up. Meanwhile turn on the oven to 275°F/140°C/Gas 1 and warm the utensils. Mix the yeast with a tablespoon of sugar in a jug. Add ½ cup warm water and allow the yeast to ferment for 10 minutes. Cream the butter and the rest of the sugar by beating together in a large mixing bowl until smooth. Beat in 2 eggs, one at a time and mix well. Gradually add the warm milk and the yeast mixture. Strain the spice water and add the liquid (½ cup) to the mixing bowl. Blend in the flour, cup by cup and make up the braided breads as in the previous recipe. Put an Easter egg in each loaf before they are set aside to rise again. Sprinkle with sesame seed. Bake the loaves as before.

Christmas Bread (*Hristópsomo*)

Like the Spicy Easter Bread, Christmas Bread is a bread of rejoicing. Make up the dough and spice liquid as for Spicy Easter Bread, but add 2 tablespoons of brandy before blending in the flour. Leave the dough in one round lump. Before the final rising take off enough to make two rolls. Cross them on the top of the dough and press on gently. Glaze the bread with butter and sprinkle with sesame seeds. Now press on some walnuts or almonds in each quarter of the dough. Bake the bread in a round cake or bread tin if your dough is very soft.

Pasta

Spaghetti with Cheese (*Spayéto me Tirí*)

Here is a basic spaghetti or macaroni recipe as made by the country people.

spaghetti *or* macaroni
salt
olive oil

pinch of basil or marjoram
grated cheese

Use 2–3 oz (50–100 g) of spaghetti or macaroni per person. Put a large pan of fresh water on to boil. Add up to 1 teaspoon of salt. When the water boils put in the pasta and cook until it is just tender. Drain in a colander or sieve. Put a tablespoon or two of oil in the pan and put the drained pasta back in. Sprinkle with herbs and mix the pasta with the oil. Serve sprinkled with any grated hard cheese. A little finely chopped garlic or some slices of tomato and green pepper may be added as a garnish. Pasta is also delicious if you sprinkle it with oil and lemon juice and garnish with some chopped parsley or coriander leaf. Add a bean dish or a nourishing soup and you have a pleasant simple meal.

Spaghetti with Mushroom and Tomato Sauce (*Spayéto me Manitári ke Domatósaltsa*)

For the sauce:

3–4 tablespoons olive oil
1 onion, chopped
a few bay leaves
1 teaspoon basil
½ cup grated carrot
6 oz (150 g) mushrooms, chopped

4 cloves garlic, finely chopped
1 teaspoon salt
pinch of freshly ground pepper
9 oz (250 g) tomatoes, chopped *or* tinned

Prepare the spaghetti as in the previous recipe, but make the sauce first. Heat the oil in a pan and fry the onion until it becomes opaque. Add the bay leaf and basil. Stir in the carrot, mushrooms and garlic and add the salt and pepper. Stir in the tomatoes. Add a little water (unless you are using tinned tomatoes, in which case use the tomato liquid) and allow to cook on a gentle heat for 15 minutes. Now prepare the spaghetti. Serve with the sauce on top. Garnish with grated cheese. A glass of wine added to the sauce instead of water will give the sauce a very appetizing taste.

This recipe is ideal for using up scraps of vegetables and may be used as a guide. Substitute chopped green beans, celery, green pepper, but do not omit the tomatoes. If you like an extra taste of tomato, add a tablespoon or two of tomato paste.

Baked Pasta with Sauce (*Pastítsio*)

Traditionally the Greeks use thin spaghetti or short macaroni in this dish, but any of your favourite pasta can be used in this dish which is somewhat like an Italian lasagne.

For the pastitsio:

1 lb (450 g) spaghetti *or* short macaroni
5 tablespoons melted butter *or* olive oil
2 tablespoons breadcrumbs
4 eggs, beaten
pasta sauce (as in the previous recipe)

3 cups white sauce (see p. 131)
3 tablespoons grated kefalotiri cheese *or* Parmesan *or* dried feta cheese
pinch of grated nutmeg

Make a sauce as in the previous recipe. Boil the pasta in a large saucepan of water until it is almost tender. Rinse in cold water and put in a bowl. Add 4 tablespoons of butter or oil, the breadcrumbs and the eggs and mix well with the pasta. Turn on the oven to 350°F/180°C/ Gas 4. Butter the sides and base of a casserole or baking pan. Put in half of the pasta. Sprinkle with a tablespoon of grated cheese and cover with half of the sauce. Cover with the rest of the pasta and another tablespoon of cheese. Spread the rest of the pasta sauce on. Pour the white sauce over. Sprinkle with more cheese and the nutmeg. Bake in the oven until the top turns golden (30–45 minutes). Cut in squares and serve with a salad.

Baked Macaroni (*Makarónia sto Fúrno*)

1 lb (450 g) macaroni
salt
½ cup melted butter *or* olive oil
5 tablespoons flour
3 cups milk
pinch of freshly ground pepper

2 cups grated kefalotiri, Parmesan
  or dried feta cheese
½ teaspoon grated nutmeg
1 tablespoon chopped parsley *or*
  coriander leaf

Boil the macaroni in a large pan of salted water until it is almost tender. Drain. Put half of the butter or oil in the pan and add the macaroni. Mix well. In a small saucepan put the rest of the butter or oil over a low heat. Gradually stir in the flour, then the milk. Sprinkle with a teaspoon of salt and some pepper. Keep on the heat for 4 or 5 minutes. Grease a casserole or baking tin and put in half of the pasta. Sprinkle half of the cheese on it. Cover with the rest of the macaroni. Pour the white sauce on. Sprinkle on the rest of the cheese and the nutmeg. Bake in the oven at 375°F/190°C/Gas 5 until the top turns golden (about 30–45 minutes). Serve garnished with fresh herbs and some salad.

Baked Macaroni with Aubergines and Courgettes (*Pastítsio Makarónia me Melitzánes ke Kolokithákia*)

1 lb (450 g) macaroni
salt
clarified butter *or* olive oil
1 onion, chopped
2–4 cloves garlic
2 cups sliced aubergine
2 cups sliced courgette
freshly ground pepper
1 teaspoon dried marjoram *or* other
  herbs

½ cup wine
1 cup chopped tomatoes
6 tablespoons flour
4 cups milk
1 teaspoon grated nutmeg
1 cup grated kefalotiri, Parmesan
  or dried feta cheese
2 eggs, beaten

Boil the macaroni in slightly salted water until it is just soft. Drain. Put 2–3 tablespoons of melted butter or olive oil in the pan and return the pasta. Turn on the oven to 350°F/180°C/Gas 4. Put two tablespoons of butter or oil in a pan and gently fry the onion until it is opaque. Add the garlic, aubergine and courgette slices and fry for 2 minutes. Sprinkle on a teaspoon of salt and some pepper. Mix well and add the dried herbs, wine and tomatoes. Mix well again and cook together for 5 minutes. In another saucepan put 6 tablespoons of melted butter or oil over a gentle heat. Stir in the flour gradually, and then the milk. Stir well until the mixture is smooth. Add the nutmeg and remove from the heat. Stir in half a cup of cheese and the beaten eggs. Grease a casserole or baking tin and put in half of the macaroni. Cover with half of the vegetable sauce. Spread the rest of the macaroni on and cover with the rest of the sauce. Pour the white sauce on and sprinkle with the rest of the cheese. Bake in the oven until the top is golden (about 30–45 minutes). Serve hot or cold with a salad.

Macaroni with Beans (*Makarónia me Fasólia*)

1 cup dried haricot *or* other dried beans	1–2 cloves garlic, finely chopped
2 tablespoons olive oil	¾ cup macaroni *or* other small pasta
1 onion, chopped	2 cups hot water
1 teaspoon salt	1 tablespoon chopped parsley *or* coriander leaf
pinch of freshly ground pepper	grated cheese
1 teaspoon marjoram *or* oregano	

Soak the beans two days before you require them, or at least overnight. Frequently change the water. Drain and add fresh water. Cook them until they are tender. Heat the oil in a frying pan and fry the onion until transparent. Add the seasoning and garlic. Stir and add to the cooked beans. Put in the dry pasta and add 2 cups of hot water. Cook the dish until the pasta is tender, adding a little more water if necessary. Serve sprinkled with green herb and grated cheese.

Pasta Salad with Dandelion (*Pastósalata me Radhíki*)

1 tablespoon olive oil	1 cup cooked beans, dry or fresh
4 oz (110 g) pasta shells, macaroni or other small pasta	1–2 cloves garlic, finely chopped
1 cup dandelion leaves, washed and shredded	2 sticks celery, sliced
	1 teaspoon marjoram *or* oregano

Add the oil to slightly salted boiling water and cook the pasta until it is tender. Drain. Mix the dandelion, beans, garlic and celery together. Gently stir in the cooked pasta. Sprinkle with dried herbs. Serve with oil and lemon sauce (see p. 130).

Pasta with Lentils (*Fakómatso*)

This is a favourite dish during the forty-day Lent fast throughout Greece, but it is also a nourishing dish to serve at any time of the year.

½ lb (225 g) noodles *or* other pasta
salt
4 tablespoons olive oil
1 cup lentils
1 onion, chopped

1–2 cloves garlic, finely chopped
2 bay leaves
1 teaspoon marjoram *or* oregano *or* basil
pinch of freshly ground pepper

Bring a large pan of water to the boil. Drop in a teaspoon of salt and 2 tablespoons of oil. Put in the noodles and boil until they are just tender (about 10 minutes). Drain. Meanwhile, put the lentils in another pan and cover with water and bring to the boil. Turn down the heat and allow the lentils to simmer. While they are cooking heat 2 tablespoons of oil in a frying pan and fry the onion until transparent. Add the garlic, bay leaves and herb. Sprinkle on a pinch of salt and pepper. Stir well and tip into the lentils. When the lentils are tender add the cooked noodles and a little more water if necessary. Cook the lentils and noodles together for 5 minutes. Serve with chunks of bread and wine.

This dish is excellent with home-made noodles (see the following recipe).

Home-made Noodles (*Hilopítes*)

2 cups flour
1 teaspoon salt

2 eggs, beaten
1 tablespoon olive oil

Sift the flour with the salt. Make a well in the centre and beat in the eggs and olive oil. Knead the dough with the hands. It may be a little sticky. Divide the dough into 3 balls and roll out on a floured board to make a thin flat sheet. Allow the sheets to stand for 15 minutes making sure they have a little dusting of flour to prevent them from sticking to the board. Roll each sheet up and slice through to make the width of noodle required. Unroll and spread them out. They can be stored for a few days if wrapped in clingfilm and kept in the refrigerator. Alternatively, dry them in a moderate oven and store in an airtight container.

Fresh noodles can be cooked straight away in boiling water and take about 10 minutes to become tender. Home-made wholewheat noodles are nourishing and filling. Added to a soup they will make a tasty and wholesome meal.

Trahana (*Trahaná*)

Another kind of Greek pasta which is used mainly in soups instead of rice or commercial pasta. Since it is made from milk or yogurt or both, it tends to be made in the autumn when there are good supplies of milk available. Like home-made wholewheat noodles, trahana is very nourishing and soon turns a soup into a filling meal. It can also be put into casseroles and stews to give added bulk and nourishment.

5 oz (140 g) yogurt
½ pint (300 ml) milk
1 tablespoon lemon juice
1 teaspoon salt
5 cups flour

Put the yogurt in a mixing bowl and beat well. Add the milk and lemon juice and stir together. Stir in the salt. Now gradually fold in the flour until a stiff dough is formed. Divide up to make 12 balls with floured hands. Lay a tea towel over a tray or board. Flatten each dough ball with the hands and put on the towel. Allow to dry for a few hours then turn over to dry on the other side. If you can put them out in the sun this is ideal. Cut the dough into small pieces and allow to continue drying until a piece will crumble easily between the fingers. They can either be crumbled like this or rubbed through a coarse sieve. The pasta is now in the form of crumbs. Wrap tightly in clingfilm and store in the refrigerator. If the trahana is allowed to dry out over a few days it can be stored in an airtight jar or tin in a cool, dry place. The recipe makes 6 cupfuls.

Rice (*Rízi*)

In front of us now is the pilaf; let our minds become pilaf.
ZORBA, *Zorba the Greek* BY NIKOS KAZANTZAKIS

Pilaf Rice (*Piláfi*)

Similar to the pulau of the Middle East and India and the risotto of
Italy, here is a recipe for basic pilaf rice. Serve it as it is with beans and
vegetables or with a tasty sauce (see Sauces, pp. 128–32). Long-grain
rice makes the best pilaf. The brown long-grain rice now on the
market is particularly good.

2 cups rice
2 tablespoons olive oil
4 cups stock
1 teaspoon salt

pinch of freshly ground pepper
1 tablespoon chopped parsley *or*
   coriander leaf

Wash the rice and leave to soak in clean water for 30 minutes. Allow to
drain. Heat the oil in a saucepan and fry the rice, stirring to prevent
sticking, until the grains become opaque. Now add the stock and salt
and pepper. Bring to the boil, cover and simmer on a low heat for

10–20 minutes. Test the rice after 10 minutes. The liquid should be absorbed and the grains tender but not mushy. Serve sprinkled with chopped herb.

To add a little more taste to this plain pilaf, fry half a chopped onion until it browns. Fry some almonds and raisins or sultanas until the sultanas puff up. Add this garnish of onion, nuts and sultanas to the rice.

Pilaf Rice with Peas (*Piláfi me Araká*)

2 cups rice
3 tablespoons olive oil
1 onion, chopped
2 bay leaves
small piece cinnamon
1 teaspoon salt
pinch of freshly ground pepper

1 cup peas (frozen *or* parboiled)
4 cups water *or* stock
1 tablespoon chopped parsley *or*
  coriander leaf
tomato slices
cucumber slices

Wash the rice and leave to soak in clean water for half an hour. Allow to drain. Heat the oil in a saucepan and fry the onion until it becomes transparent. Add the bay leaves, cinnamon, salt and pepper and rice. Cook until the rice grains become opaque, stirring from time to time. Add the peas and stir together until the peas are well coated with oil. Add 4 cups water or stock. Bring to the boil, cover and simmer over a low heat until the rice is tender (10–20 minutes). Test the rice for tenderness after 10 minutes. Serve garnished with chopped herb and tomato and cucumber slices.

This recipe would go equally well with sliced green beans or sliced courgettes. Serve with a salad or lettuce and some feta cheese.

Pilaf Rice with Egg (*Piláfi me Avgó*)

2 cups rice
3 tablespoons olive oil
1 onion, chopped
small piece cinnamon
4 cloves
1 teaspoon salt
pinch of freshly ground pepper
4 cups water *or* stock
2–4 eggs, hard-boiled and shelled

For the garnish:
2 tablespoons olive oil
1 onion, sliced
1 tablespoon blanched almonds
tomato slices
1 tablespoon chopped parsley *or*
  coriander leaf

Wash the rice and leave to soak in clean water for 30 minutes. Allow to drain. Heat the oil in a saucepan and fry the onion until it becomes transparent. Add the cinnamon, cloves, salt, pepper and rice. Cook until the rice grains become opaque, stirring to prevent the rice from sticking. Add 4 cups of water or stock. Bring to the boil, cover and simmer over a low heat until the rice is tender (10–20 minutes). Test the rice for tenderness after 10 minutes. Arrange the rice on a serving dish. Cut the eggs in slices and gently mix into the rice. Keep the rice warm in a low oven. To make the garnish, heat the olive oil in a frying pan and fry the onion until it is golden. Remove from the pan. Fry the nuts until they begin to turn golden. Arrange the tomato slices around the rice dish. Pour the fried onion and nuts onto the middle. Sprinkle with the chopped herb.

Spinach Rice (*Spanakórizo*)

2 cups rice
4 tablespoons olive oil
1 onion, chopped
1 lb (450 g) spinach, chopped

1 teaspoon salt
pinch of freshly ground pepper
pinch of ground anise

Wash the rice and allow to soak for 30 minutes. Cook in plenty of water until tender. Drain. Heat the oil and gently fry the onion for 2–3 minutes. Put in the spinach, salt and pepper and fry for 2 minutes. Mix in the cooked rice and stir well together. Spinach is best lightly cooked, but it may be cooked a little longer if preferred. Serve sprinkled with anise powder.

Tomato Rice (*Domatórizo*)

2 cups rice
4 tablespoons olive oil
1 onion, chopped
1 lb (450 g) tomatoes, chopped

2 cloves garlic, finely chopped
1 teaspoon salt
pinch of freshly ground pepper
1 teaspoon basil

Wash the rice and allow to soak for 30 minutes. Boil in slightly salted water until the rice is tender. Drain. Heat the oil in a pan and gently fry the onion for 2–3 minutes. Put in the tomatoes, garlic, salt, pepper and basil. Fry together until the tomatoes are well cooked. Mix in the cooked rice and stir well together. Serve with a salad.

Stuffed Tomatoes (*Domátes Yemistés*)

Greek tomatoes are particularly big and are ideal for stuffing. You will need the largest you can buy for this recipe.

12 large tomatoes
1 cup olive oil
2 onions, finely chopped
1 tablespoon chopped parsley
1 teaspoon basil
½ teaspoon grated nutmeg

2 teaspoons salt
½ teaspoon freshly ground pepper
2 cups cooked rice
2 tablespoons currants *or* sultanas
1 tablespoon sugar

Wash the tomatoes and cut off and retain the tops. Scoop out the pulp of each tomato and retain. Heat the oil in a pan and gently fry the onion for 2 minutes. Sprinkle the herbs, nutmeg, salt and pepper on and fry for 2 more minutes. Add the cooked rice, tomato pulp, currants and sugar and cook together for another minute. Fill each tomato with the fried filling. Place the tomatoes on a greased baking dish and add the caps. Pour a little oil on each and bake in the oven at 375°F/190°C/Gas 5 until the tomatoes are browned.

Stuffed Green Peppers
(*Piperiés Prásines Yemistés*)

6 green peppers
1 cup olive oil
2 onions, finely chopped
1 tablespoon chopped parsley *or*
   coriander leaf
1 teaspoon marjoram *or* oregano

2 teaspoons salt
½ teaspoon freshly ground pepper
4 tomatoes, chopped
2 cups cooked rice
2 tablespoons chopped walnuts *or*
   blanched almonds

Wash the peppers and cut off and retain the tops. Remove the seed and pulp from the inside and discard. Heat the oil in a pan and gently fry the onion for 2 minutes. Sprinkle on the herbs, salt and pepper. Add the tomatoes and fry together for 2 minutes. Add the cooked rice and nuts and fry together for a further 2 minutes. Fill each pepper with the fried filling. Place them on a greased baking dish and put on the caps. Pour a little oil on each and bake in the oven at 375°F/190°C/Gas 5 until the peppers are browned.

Rice Salad (*Rizósalata*)

4 courgettes
2 cups cooked rice
4 spring onions, chopped
1 small green pepper, cored and
   sliced

2 tomatoes, chopped
2 tablespoons chopped walnuts *or*
   blanched almonds
1–2 cloves garlic, finely chopped
1 lemon, cut in wedges

Boil the courgettes in a little water until they are tender. Drain and slice. Gently mix the rice, courgettes and the rest of the ingredients except the lemon. Put on a serving dish with the lemon wedges. Serve with sesame sauce (see p. 130) and salad.

Moussaka with Rice (*Musaká me Rízi*)

I owe the inspiration of this dish to Adonis who runs a small taverna in Crete in an almost permanent state of inebriation. He always puts allspice in moussaka which is a delicious spice with aubergines.

1 cup rice
1 large aubergine
salt
2 large potatoes
1 14-oz (400-g) tin tomatoes *or* equivalent
4 cloves garlic, finely chopped
1 onion, finely chopped
pinch of freshly ground pepper
1 cup olive oil
2 tablespoons clarified butter *or* margarine
2 tablespoons flour
2½ cups milk
pinch of freshly grated nutmeg
6 allspice berries

Wash the rice and leave to soak in fresh water. Cut the aubergine in rounds and soak in slightly salted water. Peel and cut the potatoes into rounds. Put the rice in a pan with the tomatoes, garlic, onion, 1 teaspoon salt and a pinch of pepper. Add 2 cups of water and allow to simmer gently until the liquid is absorbed (10–20 minutes). Dry the aubergines and deep-fry in olive oil until they just begin to turn golden. Put aside. Do the same with the potato slices. Put aside. Now make the white sauce. In a small saucepan gently heat the butter. Gradually stir in the flour, then the milk. Add a pinch of salt, pepper and nutmeg and simmer gently for 1 minute. Keep aside. Grease the sides and base of a casserole dish or baking tin. Put in a layer of potatoes, then aubergines, then a layer of savoury rice. Space out the 6 allspice berries on the top of the rice layer. Add the sauce. Bake in the oven at 375°F/190°C/Gas 5 until there is a nice golden crust on the top (about 30 minutes).

Bean Soup!

We were sitting in the bar of the Hotel Romantica. We had felt like a late snack and Dimitrios had ordered a potato omelette and some bottles of retsina. He sat twisting his moustache as I chatted about Greek food.

'They say that *amvrosía* (ambrosia) was the food of the Olympian gods.'

Dimitrios grunted and lowered his head. '*Ne.*'

'The drink of the gods was *néktar* (nectar).'

'*Ne.*'

'But no one can tell me what this food or drink is.'

Dimitrios frowned, then his eyes lit up. 'They are the most delicious food and drink you can think of!' He could see that his answer had not satisfied me and, bored with the subject, he gave a little shout and spun round in his chair. 'That man over there speaks English.' He motioned to the young man sitting at the cash desk. Dimitrios could not wait to hear some English. 'Go and speak to him,' he urged and he turned his chair so that he would be able to hear the conversation.

Perhaps he can enlighten me or even supply a recipe, I thought, and I went over to the young man. '*Miláte angliká* (Do you speak English)?' I asked him.

'Oh, ya,' he answered in a South African accent. We soon got talking and I asked him if perhaps he was good at cooking. He was not good at cooking, never had the occasion to do it, but his mother, she was a good cook. Did he know any of his mother's recipes?

'Ya, I can give you recipes. I can give you a good recipe for bean soup, you know it – *fasoládha*? Just wait a little until I'm off duty.'

We arranged to meet again the following day and I rejoined Dimitrios who was waiting for me to eat some omelette.

'What did he say?' he asked eagerly, a fork poised in the air. 'It sounded very interesting.'

'Bean soup – he can give me a recipe for bean soup.'

Dimitrios nearly choked on a piece of potato. '*"Miláte angliká?"* – *"Fasoládha!"*' he howled, clutching at his throat.

I was to discover that Greeks not only have a good sense of humour, they also have a keen appreciation of the surreal, particularly in conversation.

Soups (*Súpes*)

Hot soup comes back into favour when the autumn wind from the north or the east wind from Turkey brings the cool breezy evenings. *Fidhés* (vermicelli) is added to soups to give bulk. Serve *súpa fidhés* (vermicelli or noodle soup) with hot bread as a main course. During the strenuous forty-day fast period of Lent, such soups are essential to maintain strength.

   Where stock is mentioned in the recipes you could use fresh water, but a good home-made stock is preferable. You can also make up a stock very quickly using a vegetable stock cube. Water from boiling beans, potatoes, greens or any other vegetable will make a good stock. If you cannot use it straight away, put it in a bowl with some clingfilm over the top and keep in the refrigerator. Stockpots in Greece are often made up of various leftovers which are thrown into the pot with water and just allowed to bubble gently during the day. A good stock, of course, soon becomes a soup!

Bean Soup (*Fasoládha*)

2 cups dried beans	a few bay leaves
1 onion, chopped	1 teaspoon salt
2 carrots, peeled and sliced	pinch of freshly ground pepper
1 stick celery, sliced	1 teaspoon ground cumin seed *or*
2 tomatoes, chopped	dried sage
½ cup olive oil	3 pints (1.8 litres) stock *or* water

Soak the beans overnight in water. Next morning change the water again. Strain and cook in fresh water which just covers the beans. Bring to the boil and simmer for 10 minutes. Drain off the water. Meanwhile prepare the vegetables. In a soup pan heat the oil and gently fry the onion. Add the vegetables and seasonings. Stir well and add the beans. Make sure that all the ingredients are well covered with oil and pour the stock on. Allow to simmer until the beans and vegetables are tender.

The soup can be served quite thick. Add more water during the cooking if necessary. Serve with bread.

Bean Soup with Hot Peppers (*Fasoládha me Piperiáta*)

½ cup olive oil	1 teaspoon salt
1 onion, chopped	pinch of freshly ground pepper
1 cup sliced green beans *or* broad	½ cup small hot red or green
beans	peppers
2 carrots, chopped	3 pints (1.8 litres) stock *or* water
2 tomatoes, chopped	1 tablespoon chopped parsley *or*
2–4 cloves garlic, finely chopped	coriander leaf
1 teaspoon basil	

Heat the oil and fry the onion for 2 minutes. Add the rest of the ingredients except the hot peppers and the garnish. Mix well and fry together for 2 minutes. Add the hot peppers and cook for a further 2 minutes. If hot peppers are unavailable, ½–1 teaspoon of chilli powder may be used. Use a teaspoon of paprika powder if you do not like the pungency of chilli. This will give the red colour to the dish. Pour on the stock and cook until all the vegetables are tender. Cook the soup gently on a low heat throughout. Serve garnished with the chopped herb.

Broad Bean Soup (*Kukía Súpa*)

3 tablespoons olive oil
2 onions, chopped
3 cloves garlic, finely chopped
½ cup chopped carrot
½ lb (225 g) broad beans

½ cup chopped celery
2 teaspoons salt
½ teaspoon freshly ground pepper
1 teaspoon marjoram *or* oregano
2 pints (1.2 litres) stock *or* water

Heat the oil in a soup pan and gently fry the onion for 2 minutes. Add the garlic and vegetables and mix together. Sprinkle on the seasoning and mix again. Fry together for 5 minutes then pour the stock on. Cook on a low heat until all the vegetables are tender. Serve with bread.

A tin of tomatoes or a few chopped fresh tomatoes could be added to this soup.

Broccoli and Lentil Soup (*Brókolo ke Fakí Súpa*)

1 cup lentils
2 teaspoons salt
a few bay leaves
3 tablespoons olive oil
1 onion, chopped
1 teaspoon paprika powder

1 teaspoon cumin powder
2–4 sprigs broccoli
1 potato
1 carrot
1 teaspoon sesame seeds
1 teaspoon fennel seeds

Wash the lentils and boil in 3 pints (1.8 litres) water. Throw in the salt and bay leaves. While the lentils are gently boiling, fry the onion in a pan with the oil and stir in the paprika and cumin. Chop the broccoli sprigs and add to the fried onion. Fry for 2 minutes and add to the simmering lentils. Chop up the potato and carrot and fry in the oil (add another tablespoonful if necessary) until the vegetables are well covered with oil. Add the sesame and fennel seeds. Fry for a further 3–5 minutes and add to the lentil and broccoli soup. Cook until the vegetables are all tender and the soup is nice and thick.

Chick Pea Soup (*Revíthia Súpa*)

2 cups chick peas
½ cup olive oil
1 onion, chopped
2–4 cloves garlic, finely chopped
2 teaspoons salt
½ teaspoon freshly ground pepper

a few bay leaves
3 pints (1.8 litres) stock *or* water
1 tablespoon chopped parsley *or*
   coriander leaf
1 lemon

Soak the chick peas the day before, frequently changing the water. Rinse and change the water the next morning. Boil in fresh water for 10 minutes and discard the water. Heat the oil in a soup pan and gently fry the onion for 2 minutes. Add the garlic and chick peas and fry together for 2 minutes. Sprinkle on the seasonings and mix well. Add the stock and simmer gently until the chick peas are tender. Serve garnished with the chopped herb and slices of lemon.

   A Cretan custom is to serve this soup with bitter orange instead of lemon slices.

Egg and Lemon Soup (*Avgolémono Súpa*)

For Greeks, Easter is the most important feast of the year. Many houses will receive their annual coat of whitewash outside and a good spring-clean inside. Although some Greeks may not fast for the full forty-day period of Lent, most take the last week seriously. Even *ladheró fayitó* (food prepared with olive oil) is forbidden so that olives, vegetables, garlic and bread must sustain the people until midnight on Holy Saturday when the fast is broken. Everyone gathers in the church for the late service. There is not enough room and the little square outside becomes crowded. As it gets near midnight candles are passed around and you hand a few drachmas back for the little collection boxes. The Easter candle is lit inside the church and the blessing of light is passed from candle to candle. Bells ring overhead and fireworks and crackers are lit. Everyone embraces and shakes hands. '*Hrístos anésti!*' (Christ has risen). He has risen indeed, you reply. Good health to you, long life to you, may your fields be full! The high point of Easter has been reached. Now the long fast is over and all can go home and feast. The children will stay up for hours and young girls will jump through little bonfires while the women watch. You must eat the first meal of Easter with friends and relations gathered round the table. Usually the first dish taken will be the nourishing egg and lemon soup.

3 pints (1.8 litres) stock
½ cup rice *or* small-sized pasta
salt and pepper to taste

3 eggs
juice of 1–2 lemons

Bring the stock to the boil and add the rice. Season with salt and pepper if necessary. Allow to simmer on a gentle heat until the rice is cooked. Remove the stock from the heat. Beat the eggs well in a bowl. Beat in the lemon juice and a tablespoon of cold water. Add a cup or ladleful of hot stock gradually to the egg and lemon. Add a second cupful and stir together. Pour the mixture into the stock and stir in.

Do not allow the soup to boil now or it will curdle. Serve at once.

A nice stock which goes well with this recipe can be made by boiling cauliflower and using the thick juice for stock. Mix in a fried onion.

Leek Soup (*Práso Súpa*)

2 good-sized leeks
1 potato
1 carrot
½ cup olive oil
1 teaspoon salt

pinch of freshly ground pepper
1 teaspoon marjoram *or* oregano
1 cup yogurt
2 pints (1.2 litres) stock

Wash the vegetables, trim and chop. Heat the oil in a soup pan and fry the leeks gently for a minute. Add the potato and carrot and turn in the oil for a few minutes. Sprinkle in the seasoning. Stir in the yogurt. Add the stock and bring to the boil. Cover and simmer on a low heat for 20 minutes.

Leek and Courgette Soup (*Práso me Kolokitháki Súpa*)

3 tablespoons olive oil
1 onion, chopped
1 leek, chopped
2 courgettes, sliced
1 potato, cut in small pieces
2 tomatoes, chopped

1 teaspoon salt
½ teaspoon freshly ground pepper
2 bay leaves
1 teaspoon marjoram *or* oregano
2 pints (1.2 litres) stock

Heat the oil in a soup pan and fry the onion until it is transparent. Add the leek, courgettes, potato and tomatoes. Sprinkle with the seasoning and stir together until the vegetables are well covered with oil. Add the stock and bring to the boil. Cover and simmer over a low heat for 20–30 minutes.

Lentil Soup (*Fakí*)

2 cups lentils
3 tablespoons olive oil
1 onion, finely chopped
2 cloves garlic, finely chopped
a few bay leaves

1 teaspoon salt
pinch of freshly ground pepper
3 pints (1.8 litres) thin stock *or* water.

Wash the lentils and leave to soak. Heat the oil in a soup pan and gently fry the onion for 2 minutes. Add the garlic and stir in the seasoning. Drain the lentils and add to the soup pot. Stir together. Add the stock and bring to the boil. Simmer gently until the lentils are soft. As the lentils cook remove any frothy scum with a spoon. Lentils cook quite quickly and the soup can be served once they are tender or allow the lentils to break down to form a purée. Add more water or stock if the soup begins to dry up before the lentils are cooked.

This soup is excellent if some red wine or wine vinegar is added according to taste.

Mushroom Soup (*Manitári Súpa*)

Mushrooms contain more minerals than meat and more protein than any other vegetable except certain legumes.

2 tablespoons olive oil
1 onion, chopped
8 oz (225 g) mushrooms, sliced
salt and pepper to taste

1 teaspoon thyme *or* marjoram
1 cup yogurt
2 pints (1.2 litres) stock

Heat the oil in a soup pan and fry the onion for 2 minutes. Add the mushrooms and sprinkle in the seasoning. Cook together for 2 minutes. Add the yogurt and mix well. Pour in the stock and bring to the boil. Cover and simmer for 10–20 minutes.

Onion Soup (*Krommídhi Súpa*)

2 tablespoons olive oil
2 onions, chopped
2 cloves garlic, finely chopped
1 potato, chopped
1 teaspoon salt
pinch of freshly ground pepper

a few bay leaves
½ teaspoon marjoram *or* oregano
1 cup yogurt
2 pints (1.2 litres) stock
1 tablespoon chopped parsley *or*
  coriander leaf

Heat the oil in a soup pan and gently fry the onion for 2 minutes. Add the garlic, potato and seasoning and stir together. Add the yogurt and mix well. Pour the stock on the mixture. Bring to the boil, cover and simmer for 20 minutes. Serve garnished with chopped herb.

Potato Soup (*Patáta Súpa*)

2 tablespoons olive oil
1 onion, chopped
2 potatoes, chopped
1 carrot, chopped
1 teaspoon salt
pinch of freshly ground pepper

1 teaspoon marjoram *or* oregano
½ teaspoon ground aniseed *or*
   fennel seed
1 cup yogurt
2 pints (1.2 litres) stock
2 teaspoons chopped mint leaves

Heat the oil in a soup pan and gently fry the onion for 2 minutes. Add the potato and carrot. Sprinkle with the seasoning and fry together until the vegetables are well covered with oil. Add the yogurt and stir well. Pour the stock into the mixture and bring to the boil. Cover and simmer gently for 20 minutes. Serve sprinkled with chopped herb.

Other ways to serve this soup are to add the juice of ½ lemon or 1–2 tablespoons of tomato paste 5 minutes before serving.

Potato and Fruit Soup (*Patáta me Frúta Súpa*)

This is a way of adding interest as well as nourishment to a filling potato soup.

2 tablespoons lentils
2 tablespoons olive oil
1 onion, chopped
1 potato, chopped
½ cup dried apricots, figs *or* other
   dried fruit

1 teaspoon salt
pinch of freshly ground pepper
2 pints (1.2 litres) stock
1 tablespoon chopped parsley *or*
   coriander leaf

Wash the lentils and allow to drain. Heat the oil in a soup pan and gently fry the onion for 2 minutes. Add the potato and mix well with the oil. Add the drained lentils and fruit. Stir together and fry for 2 minutes. Sprinkle in the seasoning. Add the stock and bring to the boil. Cover and simmer for 20 minutes. Serve sprinkled with the chopped herb.

Sesame Soup (*Tahinósupa*)

3 pints (1.8 litres) stock
1 cup sesame paste
½ cup water

juice of 1 lemon
1 tablespoon chopped parsley *or*
   coriander leaf

Bring the stock to the boil slowly. Meanwhile beat the sesame paste with ½ cup of water and the lemon juice in a bowl. Add a cup of the hot stock and stir together. Remove the stock from the heat and pour in the sesame paste mixture. Garnish with the chopped herb and serve with bread.

This is a simple Lenten dish, avoiding the use of olive oil which is forbidden during the final week.

Spinach and Courgette Soup
(*Spanáki ke Kolokitháki Súpa*)

3 tablespoons olive oil
1 onion, chopped
1 teaspoon salt
pinch of freshly ground pepper
1 teaspoon ground aniseed *or* fennel seed

4 oz (110 g) spinach, chopped
2 courgettes, sliced
2 tablespoons chopped parsley *or* coriander leaf
2 pints (1.2 litres) stock

Heat the oil in a soup pan and fry the onion for 2 minutes. Sprinkle with the seasoning and add the spinach, courgettes and parsley. Stir together and fry for 2 minutes. Add the stock and bring to the boil. Cover and simmer for 10–20 minutes.

Spinach and Lentil Soup
(*Fakí me Spanáki Súpa*)

1 lb (450 g) spinach
1 cup lentils
a few bay leaves
3 tablespoons olive oil
1 bunch spring or green onions, sliced

1–2 cloves garlic, finely chopped
½ teaspoon cumin powder
½ teaspoon salt
pinch of freshly ground pepper
water *or* stock as required

Chop the spinach, wash and allow to drain. Boil the lentils in 4 cups of water with the bay leaves until they are soft. Heat the oil in a pan and gently fry the green onion for 2 minutes. Add the garlic, seasoning and drained spinach. Mix well and put in with the lentils. Add another pint of water or stock and cook for a further 15 minutes.

This soup is popular in Greece when the first young spinach leaves are available in spring.

Squash Soup (*Kolokitháki Súpa*)

2 lb (900 g) courgettes, marrow *or*
  pumpkin
2 tablespoons sugar
2 teaspoons salt
2 cups water

2 pints (1.2 litres) stock
2 teaspoons dill seed *or* coriander
  seed
½ teaspoon freshly ground pepper
1 cup yogurt

Slice the courgettes or peel and slice the marrow or pumpkin. Boil the squash with sugar and salt in 2 cups of water until just soft. Put through a sieve or purée in a blender. Add the stock and dill seed and stir well. Sprinkle in the pepper and bring to the boil. Remove from the heat and stir in the yogurt. Serve with bread and lemon slices.

Summer Vegetable Soup (*Hortósupa Kalokeriní*)

3 tablespoons olive oil
1 onion, chopped
3 cloves garlic, finely chopped
½ cup peas
½ cup green beans, sliced
2 courgettes, sliced
2 tomatoes, chopped

2 teaspoons salt
½ teaspoon freshly ground pepper
1 teaspoon chopped mint leaf
1 teaspoon basil
3 pints (1.8 litres) stock *or* water
lemon slices
cucumber slices

Heat the oil in a soup pan and gently fry the onion for 2 minutes. Add the garlic and vegetables. Mix well with the oil. Sprinkle in the seasoning and herbs and cook together for 5 minutes. Add the stock and bring to the boil. Simmer gently until all the vegetables are tender. Serve with slices of lemon and cucumber.

Tomato Soup (*Domatósupa*)

This soup is made in summer time when plenty of ripe tomatoes are available. Tinned tomatoes may be used.

4 tablespoons olive oil
1 onion, chopped
2 lb (900 g) tomatoes, chopped
1 potato, chopped
1 courgette, sliced
1 teaspoon salt

½ teaspoon freshly ground pepper
1 teaspoon sugar
3 pints (1.8 litres) thin stock *or*
  water
1 tablespoon chopped parsley *or*
  coriander leaf

Heat the oil in a soup pan and gently fry the onion for 2 minutes. Add the tomatoes and other vegetables and mix well with the oil. Sprinkle with the salt, pepper and sugar. Add the stock and bring to the boil. Simmer gently until the potatoes are quite soft. Serve garnished with the chopped herb.

Tomato Soup with Pasta
(*Domatósupa me Pásta*)

3 tablespoons olive oil
1 small onion, chopped
1 lb (450 g) tomatoes, chopped
1 carrot, sliced
1 stick celery, sliced
1 teaspoon salt
½ teaspoon freshly ground pepper

1 teaspoon basil
3 pints (1.8 litres) stock
1 cup small pasta *or* broken
  vermicelli
1 tablespoon chopped parsley *or*
  coriander leaf

Heat the oil in a soup pan and gently fry the onion for 2 minutes. Add the tomatoes, carrot and celery. Mix well with the oil. Sprinkle in the seasoning and stir together. Fry for 3 minutes. Add the stock and bring to the boil. Simmer for 10 minutes then add the pasta. When the pasta is tender the soup can be served. Serve garnished with the chopped herb.

Trahana Soup (*Trahaná Súpa*)

This is a traditional soup still made in Greek villages. The basic elements are a stock to which is added the nourishing Greek pasta *trahaná* (see p. 57). You can add vegetables, cheese and herbs to make the dish more filling or to adjust the taste. Like all simple village cookery, here is plenty of scope for the adventurous cook.

3 pints (1.8 litres) stock
salt and pepper to taste
1 teaspoon dried herbs
1 cup trahana

2 tablespoons olive oil or butter
1 tablespoon chopped parsley *or*
  coriander leaf

Bring the stock to the boil. Add seasoning to taste. Add the trahana and simmer on a low heat for 20–30 minutes. Stir in the oil and serve garnished with the chopped herb.

   Greek farmers and fishermen often start the day with a bowl of trahana soup, some olives and cheese. Other tasty additions to trahana soup could be wine, tomato paste and grated hard cheese.

Winter Soup with Beans
(*Súpa Lahanikí me Fasólia*)

2 carrots, chopped
2 sticks celery, sliced
4 tomatoes, chopped
1 potato, chopped
½ cup macaroni *or* small pasta
3 pints (1.8 litres) water
1 cup parboiled red beans
2 cloves garlic, finely chopped

1–2 teaspoons marjoram *or*
   oregano
2 teaspoons salt
½ teaspoon freshly ground pepper
2 tablespoons olive oil
1 tablespoon chopped parsley *or*
   coriander leaf

Put the vegetables in a soup pan with the pasta. Add the water and bring to the boil. Turn down the heat and simmer gently for 5 minutes. Add the rest of the ingredients except the oil and green garnish. Continue cooking until the beans and vegetables are all tender. Stir in the olive oil and garnish with the green herb. Serve with lightly toasted chunks of bread.

Yogurt Soup (*Yaúrti Súpa*)

10 oz (280 g) yogurt
2 pints (1.2 litres) water
2 tomatoes, sliced and chopped
2 cloves garlic, finely chopped

½ teaspoon salt
pinch of freshly ground pepper
a few mint leaves

Beat the yogurt in a mixing bowl and make up to 2 pints (1.2 litres) with water. Mix well. Stir in the rest of the ingredients except the mint leaves which are arranged on the top of the soup as a garnish. Chill and serve with bread, olives, cucumber and lemon.

Legumes (Óspria)

Since leguminous plants produce fruits which are extremely rich in proteins, they have a special chapter in this book. Along with cereals, they also contain fibre which ensures good digestion and they form an essential part of vegetarian diet. Like cereals, they can be easily dried and stored to provide a convenient source of protein for use at any time of the year.

When the seed beans and peas are ready to be sown the priest (*papá*) may be called to bless the seed, the sower and the land itself. The priest is essential to village life since hardly any function can begin without him. His role is very close to that seen in the Orient, particularly India. He blesses the foundation stone of every new home or important building. People starting a new business, or indeed before commencing an important journey, will seek his blessing and schools cannot open without his performance of the *ayasmó* (blessing with holy water). The land and the implements that work it are likewise blessed. He can say a mass for a good crop, for good weather and to end a period of drought.

Bean Stew (*Fasólia Yahní*)

½ cup olive oil
2 onions, chopped
2–4 cloves garlic, finely chopped
2 lb (900 g) runner beans, trimmed
  and sliced
1 lb (450 g) tomatoes, chopped

1 tablespoon sugar
1 teaspoon salt
½ teaspoon freshly ground pepper
1 teaspoon basil
2 cups hot water *or* stock

Heat the oil in a pan and gently fry the onion for 2 minutes. Add the garlic and fry together. Add the rest of the ingredients and the seasoning and mix together well. Fry for 5 minutes and then add 2 cups of hot water or stock. Simmer until the beans are tender. Serve hot or cold.

Bean Stew with Aubergines and Courgettes (*Fasólia Yahní me Melitzánes ke Kolokithákia*)

8 oz (225 g) red beans
4 tablespoons olive oil
1 onion, chopped
1 large aubergine, cut in small
  pieces
2 courgettes, sliced

2 teaspoons salt
½ teaspoon freshly ground pepper
1–2 teaspoons basil, marjoram *or*
  oregano
2–4 cloves garlic, finely chopped
2 tomatoes, chopped

Wash and soak the beans the day before they are needed. Change the water at night and the following morning. Drain and cover with fresh water. Bring to the boil and simmer for 30 minutes. Meanwhile heat the oil in a pan and fry the onion for 3 minutes. Add the aubergines and courgettes and sprinkle with the seasoning. Mix together well so that the vegetables are well covered with oil. Drain the beans but keep the stock. Add the beans, garlic and tomatoes to the frying aubergines. Mix well and add 2 cups of the bean stock. Cover and allow the stew to simmer until the beans are tender. Add more bean stock or vegetable stock to ensure a good sauce.

Other squashes such as marrow or pumpkin could be used in this dish. They make a nice contrast in texture with the beans.

Bean Moussaka (*Kukía Musaká*)

2 cups cooked broad beans *or* dried
  beans
4 tomatoes, chopped
4 cloves garlic, finely chopped
1 onion, finely chopped
salt
½ teaspoon pepper
1–2 teaspoons sage *or* other dried
  herb
2 cups water *or* stock

1 large aubergine
2 large potatoes
1 cup olive oil
2 tablespoons clarified butter *or*
  margarine
2 tablespoons flour
2½ cups milk
pinch of freshly grated nutmeg
6 allspice berries

Put the beans in a pan with the tomatoes, garlic, onion, a teaspoon of salt, pepper and herbs. Add 2 cups of water or stock and allow to simmer for 10 minutes. Meanwhile cut the aubergine and potato in round slices. Keep the aubergine in slightly salted water. Dry the aubergine slices and deep-fry in olive oil until they begin to turn golden. Do the same with the potato slices. Keep on one side. Now make the white sauce. In a small saucepan gently heat the butter. Gradually stir in the flour, then the milk. Add a pinch of salt, pepper and nutmeg and simmer gently for 1 minute. Grease the sides and base of a casserole dish or baking tin. Put in a layer of potatoes, then aubergines, then the bean mixture. Space out the allspice berries on the bean mixture. Cover with sauce. Bake in the oven at 375°F/190°C/Gas 5 until there is a golden crust on the top (about 30 minutes).

Broad Beans with Chick Peas
(*Kukía me Revíthia*)

½ lb (225 g) chick peas
½ lb (225 g) broad beans
½ cup olive oil
1 onion, chopped
1 teaspoon cumin powder
2 sticks celery, sliced

4 tomatoes, chopped
2–4 cloves garlic, finely chopped
1 teaspoon salt
½ teaspoon freshly ground pepper
1 teaspoon marjoram *or* oregano

Soak the chick peas the day before you need them. Change the water at night and the following morning. Drain and cook in fresh water until they are just tender. Drain and keep on one side. Meanwhile cook the broad beans in water until they are nearly tender, drain and keep the stock. Heat the oil in a pan and gently fry the onion until it is transparent. Add the cumin powder and stir well. Add the celery, tomatoes, garlic and seasoning and cook together for 5 minutes. Add the peas and beans and a cup of bean stock or water and cook until the beans and peas are quite tender. Add more stock or water if necessary to make a sauce.

Broad Bean Stew (*Kukía Yahní*)

2 lb (900 g) broad beans
½ cup olive oil
4 spring onions, chopped
1 lb (450 g) tomatoes, chopped
1 tablespoon chopped parsley *or* coriander leaf
1 teaspoon chopped mint leaf

1 teaspoon brown sugar
2 teaspoons basil *or* chopped dill leaf
1 teaspoon salt
½ teaspoon freshly ground pepper
2 cups water *or* stock

Shell the beans. Heat the oil in a pan and gently fry the onions for 2 minutes. Add the rest of the ingredients and the beans and stir together well. Fry for 5 minutes. Add 2 cups of water or stock and cook on a low heat until the beans are tender. Add a little more water if necessary to make a sauce. Serve hot or cold.

Broad Beans with Artichokes (*Kukía me Angináres*)

The artichoke commonly used in Greece is the small global variety which has a most delicate flavour. Do not substitute with Jerusalem or Chinese artichoke which are not the same vegetable. Artichokes are best used when quite small when almost the whole head can be eaten.

6 globe artichokes
lemon
sugar
salt
1 cup olive oil
6 spring onions, chopped

1 lb (450 g) broad beans, shelled
2 tablespoons chopped parsley *or* coriander leaf
1 teaspoon chopped mint leaf
½ teaspoon freshly ground pepper

Prepare the artichokes by removing the tough outer leaves. Trim the top with a sharp knife and leave about 1 inch (2 cm) of stem. When the artichoke is young and tender the underdeveloped hairy choke need not be removed. In older ones this must be cut out along with any spiny leaves. Put in a bowl of water which has been mixed with ½ teaspoon of salt and the juice of ½ lemon. Heat the oil in a pan and gently fry the beans, onions and herbs for 10 minutes. Drain the artichokes and put them in upside down. Sprinkle on the juice of ½ lemon, sugar, salt and pepper. Add enough water to just cover. Cover the pan and simmer gently until the beans and artichokes are tender (30–45 minutes). Sprinkle on more seasoning to taste. If you use the lemon water in which the artichokes were soaking, do not add any more lemon juice.

Peas go very well in this recipe. Frozen peas could be added 10 minutes before the end of the cooking.

This dish can be made into a salad by allowing it to cool and serving with oil and lemon dressing (see p. 130).

Broad Bean Salad (*Kukía Saláta*)

8 oz (225 g) broad beans, shelled
4 tablespoons olive oil
2 tablespoons vinegar
½ teaspoon salt
pinch of freshly ground pepper

2 spring onions, finely sliced
2 cloves garlic, finely chopped
1 tablespoon chopped parsley *or* coriander leaf

Boil the beans in slightly salted water until they are tender. Drain and allow to cool. Blend the oil and vinegar together with the salt and pepper. Stir in the onion and garlic. Put the beans in a serving dish and pour the oil and vinegar dressing on. Sprinkle with chopped herbs.

Dried beans can be treated in the same way. Soak them overnight and cook the next day. Allow to cool before adding the dressing. Dried herbs like sage, marjoram or oregano can be used in the dressing.

Chick Pea Rolls (*Burekákia apo Revíthia*)

2 cups cooked chick peas
3 tablespoons olive oil
1 onion, finely chopped
1 tomato, chopped
1 teaspoon salt
½ teaspoon freshly ground pepper
½ cup wine

½ cup crumbled feta cheese
1 tablespoon chopped parsley *or* coriander leaf
1 egg, beaten
1 lb (450 g) fillo pastry
clarified butter *or* olive oil

Mash the chick peas. Heat the oil in a pan and gently fry the onion until transparent. Add the tomato, salt and pepper and stir together. Add the wine and cook for 5 minutes. Add the cheese, parsley and beaten egg and mashed chick peas. Mix together well over the low heat for 2 minutes. Remove from the heat. Turn on the oven to 375°F/190°C/ Gas 5. Cut the pastry into sheets about 6 × 12 inches (15 × 30 cm) on a pastry board. Keep a little melted butter or oil nearby in a cup. Brush each sheet with butter. Put a spoonful of filling at one end. Fold over the sides of the pastry and roll up. Put the rolls, with the open end underneath, on a greased baking sheet and bake in the oven until crisp and golden (15–20 minutes).

Chick Pea Salad (*Revíthia Saláta*)

3 tablespoons olive oil
juice of 1 lemon
1 teaspoon salt
pinch of freshly ground pepper

2 cups cooked chick peas
1 small onion, cut in rings
1 tablespoon chopped parsley *or* coriander leaf

Stir the oil, lemon juice, salt and pepper together. Put the chick peas in a serving dish and add the oil and lemon. Decorate with the onion and parsley. Serve with a salad and yogurt.

Other dried beans could be treated in the same way.

Chick Pea Patties (*Revithokeftédhes*)

1 potato
1 cup cooked chick peas
1 onion, finely chopped
1 teaspoon salt
½ teaspoon freshly ground pepper
½ teaspoon marjoram *or* oregano

2 tablespoons chopped parsley *or* coriander leaf
1 egg, beaten
flour
olive oil for frying
lemon

Boil the potato until soft. Peel and mash. Mash the chick peas and mix in a bowl with the onion and potato. Sprinkle with the seasoning and green herb. Add the beaten egg and mix well. Shape the mixture into egg-sized balls and gently flatten. Roll in flour. Put a little oil in a frying pan and gently fry the patties until they are golden on both sides. Serve with slices of lemon.

Chick pea patties are delicious with a sauce (see Sauces, pp. 128–32) and salad.

Stuffed Chick Pea Balls (*Revithokeftédhes Yemistés*)

Make up the patty mixture as in the previous recipe. Roll the mixture into walnut-sized balls. Fry 2 tablespoons of finely chopped nuts and a finely chopped clove of garlic in a little oil. Add 1 teaspoon of fresh mint leaf. Make a small depression in each ball and stuff with the nut mixture. Roll up and fry as before. Serve with slices of lemon.

Chick Peas with White Sauce
(*Revíthia me Áspri Sáltsa*)

2 cups chick peas
3 tablespoons olive oil
1 onion, chopped
2 tomatoes, chopped
2–4 cloves garlic, finely chopped

1 cup wine
1 teaspoon basil
1 teaspoon salt
pinch of freshly ground pepper
1 cup white sauce (see p. 131)

Soak the chick peas the day before required. Change the water at night and again the following morning. Drain and boil in fresh water until tender. Heat the oil in a pan and gently fry the onion until transparent. Add the cooked peas, tomatoes, garlic, wine, basil, salt and pepper. Cook together for 5 minutes. Add the white sauce and mix well. Cook for another 5 minutes and serve.

Chick Pea Stew (*Revíthia Yahní*)

1½ cups chick peas
½ cup rice
1 carrot, sliced
1 onion, chopped
2–4 cloves garlic, finely chopped
salt and pepper to taste

a few bay leaves
1 teaspoon marjoram *or* oregano
2 cups stock
4 tomatoes, chopped
1 lb (450 g) chopped broccoli *or* sliced green beans

Soak the chick peas the day before required. Change the water at night and the following morning. Drain and boil in fresh water until tender. Meanwhile wash the rice and leave to soak for 30 minutes. Cook in boiling water until tender. Drain. Put the carrot, onion, garlic and seasoning in a stew pan. Add the stock and bring to the boil. Simmer for 10 minutes. Add the tomatoes and broccoli and simmer until the broccoli is just tender. Stir in the cooked peas and rice and allow to heat through. Add more stock or water if necessary.

Chick Pea Stew with Pasta
(*Revíthia Yahní me Pásta*)

1½ cups chick peas
3 tablespoons olive oil
1 onion, chopped
2–4 cloves garlic, finely chopped
4 tomatoes, chopped
1½ teaspoons salt
½ teaspoon freshly ground pepper

1 teaspoon sage *or* other dried herb
1 teaspoon basil
4 cups stock *or* water
½ cup small pasta
½ cup grated hard cheese
1 tablespoon chopped parsley *or* coriander leaf

Soak the chick peas the day before required. Change the water at night and the following morning. Drain and boil in fresh water until just tender. Drain. Heat the oil in a stew pan and gently fry the onion until transparent. Add the garlic, tomatoes, seasoning, herbs and chick peas. Stir together well. Fry for 3 minutes. Add the stock and the pasta. Simmer until the pasta is tender. Sprinkle on the cheese and garnish with the chopped herb.

Chick Peas with Apricots
(*Revíthia me Veríkokka*)

2 cups cooked chick peas
½ cup olive oil
1 onion, chopped
2–4 cloves garlic, finely chopped
2 teaspoons salt
½ teaspoon freshly ground pepper
2 teaspoons marjoram *or* oregano

1 teaspoon cumin powder
1 14-oz (400-g) tin tomatoes *or*
   fresh tomatoes, chopped
½ lb (225 g) dried apricots
1 tablespoon chopped parsley *or*
   coriander leaf
water *or* stock as required

Drain the chick peas. In a pan heat the oil and gently fry the onion for 2 minutes. Add the chick peas, garlic, seasoning, tomatoes and apricots. Stir together and fry for 5 minutes. Add 2 cups of water and allow to simmer until the apricots are tender. Add more water or stock if necessary. Serve garnished with the chopped herb.

This dish is excellent when served with lemon juice, yogurt and lettuce.

Green Bean Stew (*Fasulákia Fréska Yahní*)

1 lb (450 g) fresh green beans
½ cup olive oil
1 onion, chopped
4 tomatoes, chopped
1 teaspoon salt

pinch freshly ground pepper
pinch cumin powder
1 tablespoon chopped parsley *or*
   coriander leaf

Wash the beans and trim. Slice. Heat the oil in a pan and gently fry the onion until transparent. Add the beans, tomatoes, salt, pepper and cumin powder. Fry together for 5 minutes and add a cup of water. Cook until the beans are tender, adding a little more water if necessary. Serve garnished with the chopped herb.

Lentils and Rice (*Fakí ke Rízi*)

1 cup lentils	1 onion, chopped
1 cup rice	4 cloves garlic, finely chopped
1 pint (600 ml) water	1 teaspoon salt
2 tablespoons olive oil	pinch of freshly ground pepper

Wash the lentils and rice. Bring a pint (600 ml) of water to the boil and add the lentils and rice. Allow to simmer. Meanwhile heat the oil in a frying pan and gently fry the onion and garlic. Season with salt and pepper. Pour into the lentils and rice. Cook until they are both tender, adding more water if necessary to make a thick sauce.

Lentil Salad (*Fakí Saláta*)

2 cups lentils	pinch of freshly ground pepper
1 small onion *or* 3 spring onions, chopped	1 teaspoon marjoram *or* oregano
	1 tablespoon vinegar
4 tomatoes, chopped	2 tablespoons olive oil
4 slices cucumber, chopped	1 tablespoon chopped parsley *or*
1 teaspoon salt	coriander leaf

Wash the lentils and boil in slightly salted water until just soft. Do not allow the lentils to cook longer or they will break down to a pulp and become soup. Drain. Keep the liquid for stock. Mix the lentils with the onion, tomato and cucumber. Sprinkle with salt, pepper and the marjoram or oregano. Add the vinegar and oil and mix gently. Serve sprinkled with chopped herb.

Mixed Bean Salad (*Fasólia Anámikta Saláta*)

2 cups mixed dried beans	4 tablespoons olive oil
1 cup sliced fresh green beans	1 teaspoon salt
½ onion, finely chopped	pinch of freshly ground pepper
2 cloves garlic, finely chopped	1 teaspoon chopped mint leaf
2 tablespoons vinegar	

Soak the beans the day before required. Change the water at night and the following morning. Drain. Boil in fresh water until soft. Drain. Meanwhile cook the fresh beans in a little boiling water until tender. Drain. Keep the fresh bean water for stock. Put all the beans in a serving bowl and mix with the onion, garlic, vinegar and oil. Sprinkle on the salt, pepper and mint leaf. Mix again.

Yogurt may be substituted for the vinegar and oil dressing. A mixture of sesame paste, water and lemon juice also makes a nice dressing for this salad.

Serve with fresh tomatoes and wedges of lemon.

Peas in White Sauce (*Pizélia me Áspri Sáltsa*)

2 lb (900 g) fresh peas
4 tablespoons olive oil
4 spring onions, chopped
2 tablespoons flour
1 tablespoon lemon juice
1 teaspoon salt

1 teaspoon sugar
pinch of freshly ground pepper
1 tablespoon chopped parsley *or* coriander leaf
2 tomatoes, sliced

Cook the peas in boiling water until almost tender. Drain but keep the water. Heat the oil in a pan and gently fry the onion until soft. Stir in the flour. Do not let it brown. Remove from the heat and gradually add 2 cups of pea water, stirring all the time. Heat again and cook for 2 minutes. Add the lemon juice, salt, sugar and pepper. Stir in the peas and cook for 5 minutes. Serve sprinkled with the chopped herb and arrange the tomato slices round the edge of the dish.

Vegetables (*Lahaniká*)

Vegetables play an important part in a Greek meal. They are nearly always eaten cold or lukewarm with a dressing of oil and lemon or oil and vinegar. Some people like to eat their cooked vegetables while they are still hot and in winter this is quite acceptable. A wide variety of vegetables are grown, but many of them have a short season. Thus dishes reflect this seasonal change so that what may be cooked one month will be substituted by a different dish the next.

The Greek use of green vegetables is particularly characteristic and should recommend itself to vegetarians since wild greens as well as cultivated ones feature in the cuisine. All these vegetables come under the generic Greek term of *hórta*. Dandelion leaves (*radhíkia*) are very popular and several varieties are cultivated for sale in local markets. Wild varieties are considered more of a delicacy. Gather the leaves when young and tender, before the plant breaks into its bright yellow flowers. The yellow flowering weed *vrúva*, known as charlock or field mustard (*Sinapis arvensis*) is another delicacy favoured by Greeks. Again, gather the plant before it flowers. Wild greens may be prepared like the recipe for Dandelion Salad in this book (see p. 109).

Greek cooks do not like to throw away the green tops of root vegetables. Turnip, radish and beetroot tops are excellent if gently boiled and eaten cold with a dressing of olive oil and lemon juice.

Ladheró fayí (vegetables cooked in olive oil) are left to cool before eating. This allows the oil to combine with the moisture given off by the vegetables. This is simply the Greek style and it goes well with a hot dry climate, but if you live in a colder, wetter climate, you may prefer to keep your cooked vegetables hot!

Artichokes with Tomatoes (*Angináres me Domátes*)

6–8 small globe artichokes
lemon
salt
½ cup olive oil
1 onion, chopped

4 tomatoes, chopped
1 teaspoon salt
½ teaspoon freshly ground pepper
1 teaspoon basil
1 cup stock

Trim the artichokes by cutting off the stems and the tough outside leaves. Cut them in half and trim out any fuzzy centres. Keep in a bowl of water which has ½ teaspoon salt and 1 tablespoon lemon juice in while you are trimming. Heat the oil in a pan and gently fry the onion for 2 minutes. Drain the artichokes and fry with the onion until they begin to turn golden. Add the tomatoes, salt, pepper and basil and fry for 2 minutes. Add the stock and simmer until the artichokes are tender, using a little more stock or water if necessary (20–30 minutes).

Artichokes with Potatoes (*Angináres me Patátes*)

6–8 small globe artichokes
½ cup olive oil
2 onions, chopped
1 teaspoon salt
½ teaspoon freshly ground pepper

1 lb (450 g) small potatoes
½ lb (225 g) small carrots
2 tablespoons chopped dill leaf *or*
　other green herb
1 tablespoon flour

Trim the artichokes by cutting off the stems and the tough outside leaves. Cut them in half and trim out any fuzzy centres. Put upside down in a pan and add the oil. Sprinkle on the onion and fry together over a gentle heat for 5 minutes. Sprinkle on the salt and pepper and mix well. Peel and wash the potatoes and carrots and cut in small pieces. Put in with the artichokes. Sprinkle with the chopped herb and add enough water to just cover the vegetables. Simmer until the artichokes are tender. Mix the flour with a cup of hot water and add to the dish.
　Greeks sometimes eat this dish cold.

Stuffed Artichokes (*Anginâres Yemistés*)

8 globe artichokes
juice of 1 lemon
1 teaspoon salt
3 tablespoons olive oil
1 onion, finely chopped
2–4 cloves garlic, finely chopped
1 tablespoon breadcrumbs

½ cup chopped walnuts *or*
  almonds
pinch of freshly ground pepper
1 tablespoon chopped parsley *or*
  coriander leaf
white sauce (see p. 131)
grated hard cheese

Trim off the stems of the artichokes and remove the tough outer leaves. Trim off the tops and remove the hairy chokes from the centre. Put them in a pan with just enough water to cover. Add the lemon juice and salt and simmer until the artichokes are tender (20–30 minutes). Drain. Heat the oil in a pan and gently fry the onion for 2 minutes. Add the garlic, breadcrumbs, nuts, pepper and chopped herb. Fry together for 5 minutes. Use this mixture to stuff the artichokes. Arrange on a greased baking tray and pour some white sauce over each stuffed artichoke. Sprinkle on a little grated cheese and bake in the oven at 375°F/190°C/Gas 5 until golden (20–30 minutes).

Aubergine Pie (*Melitzanópitta*)

olive oil
1 onion, chopped
4 tomatoes, chopped
2–4 cloves garlic, finely chopped
1 teaspoon salt
½ teaspoon freshly ground pepper
1 teaspoon basil

1 cup yogurt
1 cup cottage or curd cheese
2 teaspoons sesame seeds
1 large aubergine
1 cup crumbled feta cheese
1 tablespoon chopped parsley *or*
  coriander leaf

Turn on the oven to 350°F/180°C/Gas 4. Heat 2 tablespoons of oil in a pan and fry the onion for 2 minutes. Add the tomatoes, garlic, salt, pepper and basil. Cook together for 5 minutes. Mix the yogurt and cheese together with the sesame seeds. Wash the aubergine and trim. Cut in thin slices. Heat half a cup of olive oil in a frying pan and fry the aubergine slices until golden. Remove and drain on absorbent paper. Fill the bottom of a greased casserole or baking dish with some of the aubergine slices. Cover with some of the tomato mixture and then with some of the yogurt and cheese mixture. Put on another layer of aubergine, tomato and cheese as before. Cover with feta cheese. Bake in the oven until the top turns golden (30–40 minutes). Serve garnished with the chopped herb.

Aubergines with Green Peppers
(*Melitzánes me Piperiés*)

½ cup olive oil
1 onion, chopped
4 cloves garlic, finely chopped
1 aubergine, cut in slices
1 green pepper, cut in slices

4 tomatoes, chopped
1 teaspoon basil
1 teaspoon salt
pinch of freshly ground pepper
2 cups water

Heat the oil in a pan and gently fry the onion for 2 minutes. Add the garlic. Put in the aubergine and green pepper and fry for 2 minutes. Add the tomatoes and seasoning and fry together for a further 2 minutes. Add 2 cups water and stew until the vegetables are tender.

Baked Aubergines (*Melitzánes sto Fúrno*)

1 large aubergine
1–2 eggs, beaten
olive oil
1 onion, chopped
4 cloves garlic, finely chopped
1 14-oz (400-g) tin tomatoes *or*
   fresh tomatoes

1 teaspoon marjoram, oregano *or*
   basil
1 teaspoon salt
pinch of freshly ground pepper
feta cheese
nutmeg *or* cinnamon

Turn on the oven to 400°F/220°C/Gas 6. Wash the aubergine and trim. Slice in half lengthwise and then slice each half. Dip each slice in the beaten egg. Heat a cup of olive oil in a pan and gently fry the aubergine slices until golden. Remove and drain on absorbent paper. Put the slices in a greased casserole or baking dish. Fry the onion until it is transparent. Add the garlic, tomatoes, herb, salt and pepper and fry together for 5 minutes. Pour this mixture over the aubergine slices. Spread slices of feta cheese over the top. Sprinkle on a little olive oil. Grind some fresh nutmeg or cinnamon over the cheese and bake the dish in the oven until the top turns golden (about 20 minutes).

Stewed Aubergines (*Melitzánes Yahní*)

1 cup olive oil
1 onion, chopped
1 large aubergine, sliced
1 teaspoon salt
½ teaspoon pepper
4 tomatoes, chopped

4 cloves garlic, finely chopped
1 teaspoon sugar
2 tablespoons wine
2 teaspoons basil
a few bay leaves
1 cup stock *or* water

Heat the oil in a pan and gently fry the onion until it is transparent. Add the aubergine slices. Sprinkle on the salt and pepper and stir together. Fry for 2 minutes. Add the rest of the ingredients and cook together gently until the aubergine is tender. Add a little more water if necessary but do not make the sauce too thin. Serve hot or cold.

Stuffed Aubergines (*Melitzánes Yemistés*)

4–6 aubergines
salt
1 lb (450 g) potatoes, cooked
½ cup olive oil
4 spring onions, sliced
1 tablespoon chopped parsley *or*
    coriander leaf

½ cup cooked rice
1 teaspoon salt
pinch of freshly ground pepper
2 tomatoes, chopped
1 teaspoon sugar

Wash the aubergines and trim off the ends. Lay the aubergine lengthwise and cut off the top. Scoop out the flesh and put the two skins in slightly salted water. Keep the flesh. Peel and mash the potatoes. Heat the oil in a pan and gently fry the onions for 2 minutes. Add the aubergine flesh, potato, parsley, rice and seasoning and stir together. Fry for 2 minutes. Add the tomatoes and sugar and cook for 5 minutes. Use this mixture to stuff the aubergines. Take out the top and bottom pieces and drain. Fill up with stuffing and put the stuffed piece on a greased baking sheet. Press on the top. Bake in the oven at 375°F/190°C/Gas 5 until the aubergines are tender and golden (about 30 minutes). Serve with tomato sauce or white sauce poured over (see pp. 130 and 131).

Aubergine Fritters (*Melitzánes Tiganítes*)

1 large aubergine
1–2 eggs, beaten
salt and pepper to taste

breadcrumbs
olive oil

Trim the aubergine and cut in slices. Beat the eggs with a little salt and pepper. Put the breadcrumbs on a plate nearby. Dip the aubergine slices in the beaten egg and roll liberally in the breadcrumbs. Heat some oil in a frying pan and fry the slices on both sides until they are golden. Drain and allow to cool. Serve with a salad.

   Aubergine fritters are delicious in pitta bread with some lettuce and slices of lemon.

Broccoli with Yogurt (*Brókolo me Yaúrti*)

1 lb (450 g) broccoli florets
3 tablespoons olive oil
1 onion, chopped
4 cloves garlic, finely chopped
1 teaspoon marjoram *or* oregano

½ teaspoon cumin powder
1 teaspoon salt
pinch of freshly ground pepper
1 cup yogurt
2 cups water

Wash and slice the broccoli. Heat the oil and gently fry the onion until transparent. Add the garlic and seasoning. Stir together and add the broccoli pieces. Fry together for 2 minutes. Add the yogurt and 2 cups of water and simmer until the broccoli is tender.

Cabbage Rolls (*Láhanodolmádhes*)

1 large green cabbage
½ cup olive oil
1 onion, chopped
2 tomatoes, chopped
2 teaspoons salt
½ teaspoon freshly ground pepper
½ cup cooked rice

1 cup cooked chick peas
1 cup toasted breadcrumbs
2 tablespoons chopped parsley
½–1 teaspoon aniseed powder
  (optional)
egg and lemon sauce (see p. 128)

Wash the cabbage and trim off any spoilt leaves. Immerse in slightly salted boiling water until the leaves soften (5–10 minutes). Remove, drain and cut off the large outer leaves ready for stuffing. Heat the oil in a pan and gently fry the onion until transparent. Add the tomatoes, salt and pepper and fry together for 2 minutes. Add the rice. Mash the chick peas and add them with the breadcrumbs. Sprinkle with the chopped herb and aniseed and mix together well. Take a cabbage leaf and put a little of the filling mixture on. Fold over the sides of the leaf and roll up. Put the rolls in a casserole with their open ends underneath. Pack them tightly. Pour on just enough water or stock to cover the rolls. Put on the lid and cook on a low heat for 30 minutes. Serve hot with egg and lemon sauce poured over the rolls.

Cauliflower Fritters (*Kunupídhi Tiganítes*)

1 cauliflower
1 teaspoon salt
1 cup flour
2 tablespoons clarified butter *or*
  margarine

2 eggs, beaten
½ cup milk
olive oil for deep-frying
lemon

Wash and trim the cauliflower and cut in pieces. Boil in water with ½ teaspoon salt until just tender. Make the batter by sifting ½ teaspoon salt with the flour. Cream in the butter. Add the beaten eggs then gradually add the milk until you have made a creamy batter. Heat the oil in a deep-frying pan. Dip the cauliflower pieces in the batter and deep-fry until golden. Allow to drain on absorbent paper. Arrange on a dish and sprinkle with lemon juice.

Cauliflower Stew (*Kunupídhi Yahnistó*)

1 cauliflower
½ cup olive oil
1 onion, chopped
1 teaspoon salt
½ teaspoon freshly ground pepper
1 teaspoon ground aniseed
2 carrots, thinly sliced

2 tomatoes, chopped
2 sticks celery, sliced
1 cup stock
1 cup yogurt
2–4 cloves garlic, finely chopped
1 tablespoon chopped parsley *or*
  coriander leaf

Wash the cauliflower and cut in small pieces. Heat the oil in a pan and fry the onion until transparent. Add the cauliflower pieces and fry until the pieces are well covered in oil and beginning to turn golden. Sprinkle with salt, pepper and aniseed. Add the carrots, tomatoes and celery. Mix well. Add the stock, yogurt and garlic. Cover and simmer until the vegetables are tender. Serve garnished with the chopped herb.

Fried Cauliflower (*Kunupídhi Tiganitá*)

1 cauliflower
½ cup olive oil
1 onion, chopped
2–4 cloves garlic, finely chopped
1 teaspoon salt
pinch of freshly ground pepper

2 tablespoons chopped almonds *or*
  other nuts
white sauce
1 tablespoon chopped parsley *or*
  coriander leaf

Wash the cauliflower and cut in small pieces. Heat the oil in a pan and fry the onion for 2 minutes. Add the garlic. Sprinkle with salt and pepper. Add the cauliflower pieces and fry until they turn golden. Remove from the pan and arrange on a serving dish. Fry the nuts for a few minutes. Sprinkle these over the cauliflower pieces. Cover with white sauce (see p. 131) and serve garnished with chopped herb.

Stewed Celery (*Sélino Yahní*)

1 bunch celery
2 tablespoons olive oil
1 onion, chopped
1 teaspoon salt
pinch of freshly ground pepper
½ teaspoon ground fennel seed *or* aniseed

2 cloves garlic, finely chopped
1 cup stock
1 tablespoon chopped parsley *or* coriander leaf
1 tablespoon sesame seeds, lightly toasted

Wash and trim the celery. Chop each stalk into a few pieces. Cook in a little boiling water for 5 minutes. Drain in a colander and keep the stock. Heat the oil in a pan and fry the onion until transparent. Put in the drained celery and turn well in the oil. Sprinkle with salt, pepper, fennel or aniseed, and garlic. Mix together. Add the stock and bring to the boil. Cover and simmer until the celery is tender. Serve sprinkled with the green herb and sesame seeds.

Stewed Courgettes (*Kolokithákia Yahní*)

2 lb (900 g) courgettes
½ cup olive oil
2 onions sliced
1 lb (450 g) tomatoes, chopped
1 teaspoon chopped mint leaves
1 teaspoon chopped dill leaves *or* marjoram

1 teaspoon brown sugar
1 teaspoon salt
pinch of freshly ground pepper
1 cup water *or* stock

Wash and trim the courgettes. Cut in half. Heat the oil in a pan and gently fry the onion for 2 minutes. Add the tomatoes, herbs and sugar and fry for 2 minutes. Put in the courgettes and sprinkle with salt and pepper. Add a cup of hot water or stock and gently stew the courgettes until tender. Serve hot or cold.

Courgettes with Egg and Lemon Sauce (*Kolokithákia me Avgolémono Sáltsa*)

2 lb (900 g) courgettes
½ cup olive oil
2 onions, chopped
2–4 cloves garlic, finely chopped
1 teaspoon mint leaves
1 tablespoon chopped parsley *or* coriander leaf
2 teaspoons salt

½ teaspoon freshly ground pepper
2 tomatoes, chopped
1 teaspoon sugar
pinch of freshly grated nutmeg
2 cups water *or* stock
2 eggs
1 teaspoon cornflour
juice of 1 lemon

Wash and trim the courgettes and cut into halves. Heat the oil in a pan and gently fry the onion for 2 minutes. Add the garlic, herbs, salt and pepper and fry for 2 minutes. Add the tomatoes, sugar, nutmeg and the courgettes. Stir together well. Add 2 cups water or stock and cook gently until the courgettes are tender. When they are almost tender make the egg and lemon sauce. Beat the eggs well. Mix the cornflour with a tablespoon of water and beat into the eggs. Beat in the lemon juice. Take a ladleful of juice from the courgette pan and slowly beat it into the sauce. Pour this sauce over the courgettes. Do not allow the liquid in the pan to boil. Serve hot.

Courgettes with Garlic Sauce (*Kolokithákia me Skordhósaltsa*)

2 lb (900 g) courgettes
6 tablespoons olive oil
½ cup almonds *or* walnuts
4–6 cloves garlic

1 teaspoon salt
2 tablespoons vinegar
1 tablespoon chopped parsley *or* coriander leaf

Wash the courgettes and slice in half lengthways. Heat 2 tablespoons of oil in a pan and lightly fry the courgettes. Remove from the pan. If using almonds, blanch by boiling in water for 1 minute then peel. Pound the nuts with the garlic and salt to make a paste. Add the rest of the oil and the vinegar gradually until the mixture is smooth. Put the courgettes on a serving dish and pour the garlic sauce over. Sprinkle with the chopped herb and serve with a salad.

Courgettes with Cheese (*Kolokithákia me Féta*)

1 lb (450 g) courgettes
½ cup olive oil
½ lb (225 g) feta cheese

2 teaspoons marjoram *or* oregano
pinch of freshly ground pepper

Wash and trim the courgettes and cut in half lengthways. Gently fry in oil until they soften. Cover with slices of cheese and put under the grill or bake in a moderate oven until the cheese begins to turn golden. Sprinkle with herbs and pepper.

Courgette Fritters (*Kolokithákia Tiganíta*)

1 lb (450 g) courgettes
1 egg, beaten
1½ tablespoons flour
pinch of baking powder

pinch of salt
pinch of freshly ground pepper
olive oil for deep-frying

Wash the courgettes and trim. Slice into thick rounds. Beat together the egg, flour, baking powder, salt, pepper and a little water to make a thick batter. Heat the oil in a deep-frying pan. Dip the courgette rounds in the batter and quickly fry in hot oil until golden. Drain on absorbent paper. Serve with a bean dish and yogurt.

Stuffed Courgettes (*Kolokithákia Yemistá*)

2 lb (900 g) courgettes
2 tablespoons olive oil
1 onion, chopped
2 cloves garlic, finely chopped
½ cup chopped nuts

1 tablespoon chopped parsley *or* coriander leaf
2 teaspoons salt
½ teaspoon freshly ground pepper
tomato sauce (see p. 130)

Wash the courgettes and trim. Slice off a thin piece along the length of each courgette. Carefully scoop out the centres. Keep the courgette flesh. Heat the oil in a frying pan and gently fry the onion for 2 minutes. Add the garlic, nuts, herb and seasoning and fry together for 1 minute. Add the courgette flesh and mix together well. Stuff the courgettes and place closely together in a casserole or baking dish. Pour the tomato sauce over and bake in the oven at 375°F/190°C/Gas 5 for 30 minutes.

This dish is also delicious when baked with egg and lemon sauce (see p. 128).

Stewed Leeks (*Práso Yahnistó*)

2 lb (900 g) leeks
2 sticks celery
1 lb (450 g) tomatoes, chopped
2 teaspoons marjoram *or* oregano

1½ teaspoons salt
½ teaspoon freshly ground pepper
2 cups water *or* stock
½ cup crumbled feta cheese

Wash the leeks, trim and cut in pieces. Put in a pan. Slice the celery and put in with the leeks. Add the tomatoes and sprinkle with the seasoning. Add 2 cups of water or stock and bring to the boil. Cover and simmer until the leeks are tender. Serve sprinkled with the cheese.

Okra Stew (*Bámies Yahnistés*)

2 lb (900 g) okras
½ cup olive oil
2 onions, chopped
1 lb (450 g) tomatoes, chopped
1½ teaspoons salt

½ teaspoon freshly ground pepper
1 cup water *or* stock
2 teaspoons sugar
1 tablespoon vinegar

Wash and trim the okras. Heat the oil in a pan and gently fry the onion for 2 minutes. Add the okras and turn in the oil until they are well covered. Add the tomatoes and sprinkle with the salt and pepper. Add a cup of water or stock, the sugar and vinegar. Stir together and simmer gently until the okras are tender.

Lemon juice may be substituted for the vinegar. Sprinkle over the dish when the okras are cooked.

Okra with Figs (*Bámies me Síka*)

1 lb (450 g) okras	4 tomatoes, chopped
1 lb (450 g) courgettes	2 teaspoons basil
1 cup olive oil	2 teaspoons salt
1 onion, chopped	½ teaspoon freshly ground pepper
1 cup dried figs	2 cups water *or* stock

Wash and trim the okras and courgettes. Slice the courgettes in half. Heat the oil in a casserole and fry the onion for 2 minutes. Add the okras, courgettes and figs and fry together for 3 minutes. Add the tomatoes and seasoning. Mix well and add 2 cups of water or stock. Cover and bake in the oven at 375°F/190°C/Gas 5 for 30 minutes, or simmer gently until the vegetables are tender.

Stuffed Peppers (*Piperiés Yemistés*)

8 green peppers	4 tomatoes, chopped
½ cup olive oil	2 teaspoons marjoram *or* oregano
1 onion, finely chopped	2 teaspoons salt
2 cloves garlic, finely chopped	½ teaspoon freshly ground pepper
1 cup cooked chestnuts	tomato sauce *or* white sauce (see
1 cup cooked chick peas	pp. 130 and 131)
1 cup cooked rice	
1 tablespoon chopped parsley *or*	
coriander leaf	

Cut off the tops of the peppers and remove the seeds. Keep the tops. Heat the oil in a pan and gently fry the onion for 2 minutes. Meanwhile mash the chestnuts and chick peas. Add the garlic to the onion. Stir in the chestnuts, chick peas and rice. Sprinkle with the chopped herb. Add the tomatoes and seasoning and fry together for 2 minutes. Stuff the peppers with the fried mixture and replace the lids. Arrange on a greased baking dish. Pour some tomato or white sauce over each pepper and bake the dish in the oven at 375°F/190°C/Gas 5 for 30–45 minutes.

Potatoes and Tomatoes (*Patátes ke Domátes*)

2 lb (900 g) peeled potatoes
½ cup olive oil
2 onions, chopped
2 teaspoons salt
½ teaspoon freshly ground pepper

a few bay leaves
1 lb (450 g) tomatoes, chopped
4 cloves garlic, finely chopped
2 teaspoons basil *or* oregano
2 cups water *or* stock

Wash the potatoes and cut in small pieces. Heat the oil in a pan and fry the onion for 2 minutes. Add the potato pieces. Sprinkle with salt, pepper and bay leaves. Fry together for 2 minutes. Add the tomatoes, garlic and basil. Pour 2 cups of water or stock into the pan, cover and cook over a gentle heat until the potatoes are tender.

Potatoes with Courgettes (*Patátes me Kolokithákia*)

1 lb (450 g) peeled potatoes, cut in
   pieces
1 lb (450 g) courgettes, trimmed
   and sliced
4 cloves garlic, finely chopped

½ cup olive oil
1 teaspoon salt
pinch of freshly ground pepper
2 teaspoons chopped mint leaf
2 cups stock

Put the potatoes and courgettes in a casserole dish and sprinkle with the garlic. Pour the oil on and mix well. Sprinkle on the seasoning. Add the stock. Cover and simmer until the potato is tender.

Cubes of marrow or pumpkin could be substituted for the courgettes.

Potatoes with Egg and Lemon Sauce (*Patátes me Avgolémono Sáltsa*)

2 lb (900 g) peeled potatoes
½ cup olive oil
2 onions, chopped
4 cloves garlic, finely chopped
2 teaspoons chopped mint leaves
1 tablespoon chopped parsley *or*
   dill leaf
2 teaspoons salt

½ teaspoon freshly ground pepper
4 tomatoes, chopped
½ teaspoon grated nutmeg
3 cups hot water *or* stock
2 eggs
1 teaspoon cornflour
juice of 1–2 lemons

Wash the potatoes and cut in pieces. Heat the oil in a pan and gently fry the onion for 2 minutes. Add the garlic, herbs, salt and pepper and cook for 2 minutes. Add the tomatoes, nutmeg and the potato pieces.

Mix together and cook for another 2 minutes. Pour 3 cups of hot water or stock into the pan and cook over a low heat until the potato is almost tender. Make the egg and lemon sauce at this point. Beat the eggs. Mix the cornflour with a tablespoon of water and beat into the eggs. Beat in the lemon juice. Take a ladleful of juice from the potato pan and slowly mix into the egg and lemon. Pour this sauce over the potatoes. Do not allow the dish to boil or the sauce will curdle.

Potato Balls (*Patáta Keftédhes*)

6 large potatoes	1 tablespoon chopped parsley *or*
olive oil	coriander leaf
1 teaspoon salt	2 eggs, beaten
½ teaspoon freshly ground pepper	flour
½ teaspoon ground cumin	lemon
3 tablespoons grated hard cheese	

Boil the potatoes until soft. Peel and mash with 2 tablespoons of olive oil. Sprinkle with the seasoning and mix together. Mix the cheese and chopped herb with the potato. Mix in the beaten egg until a stiff mixture is formed. Make into walnut-sized balls and roll in flour on a board. Fry in hot oil until the balls are golden. Serve with wedges of lemon.

These potato balls are delicious when stuffed. Fry a finely chopped onion in oil and add a tablespoon of chopped nuts. Sprinkle with half a teaspoon of marjoram or oregano and fill the potato balls with this mixture. Make a hollow and put in a little of the stuffing. Close up and roll in flour. Fry in the usual way. Serve with tomato sauce (see p. 130) and a salad.

Spinach Pie (*Spanakópitta*)

For the filling:	*For the pastry:*
2 tablespoons olive oil	1 tablespoon dried yeast
1 onion, chopped	½ cup warm water
6 spring onions, chopped	1 teaspoon sugar
1 lb (450 g) spinach, chopped	2 cups flour
2 tablespoons chopped parsley *or*	1 teaspoon salt
dill leaf	5 tablespoons olive oil
1 cup crumbled feta cheese	
½ teaspoon freshly ground pepper	

Make the filling by gently heating the oil in a pan. Add the onion and green onion and fry until they soften. Put in the spinach and cook for 5 minutes. Remove from the heat and add the rest of the ingredients. Make the pastry by adding the yeast to ½ cup of warm water. Stir in the sugar and allow the yeast to ferment for 10 minutes. It will double its volume. Sift the flour with the salt. Make a well in the centre and put in 3 tablespoons of oil. Stir in the yeast mixture. Stir together with a knife and knead the dough until it is smooth and pliable, adding a little water if necessary. Cover the dough with a cloth and keep in a warm place for the dough to double its size. Knead the dough again. Put the oven on to 375°F/190°C/Gas 5. Divide the dough in half. Roll out the two pieces to make pastry. Grease a 9-inch (23-cm) pie dish and line with one of the pastry pieces. Put the spinach filling into the dish and cover with the other piece of pastry to make a top. Flute the edges of the pastry onto the pie dish with the fingertips. Pour 2 tablespoons of oil on the top of the crust and brush over. Prick the crust to allow steam to escape during the cooking. Bake in the oven until the crust is golden.

Cretan Spinach Pie (*Spanákokalitsúnia*)

1 lb (450 g) flour
2½ teaspoons salt
4 teaspoons baking powder
8 oz (225 g) clarified butter *or* margarine
2 lbs (900 g) spinach

½ teaspoon freshly ground pepper
1 lb (450 g) mizithra *or* cottage cheese
2 eggs
4 tablespoons olive oil
sesame seeds

Sift the flour with ½ teaspoon salt and baking powder. Rub in the butter to make crumbs. Add enough water to make a soft pastry dough which is not sticky. Cover with a cloth.

Wash the spinach and chop. Put in a bowl and sprinkle with 2 teaspoons salt and pepper. Add the cheese and 1 beaten egg. Pour the oil on and mix well.

Roll out the dough to make a sheet. Cut out 5-inch (12-cm) squares. Put some of the filling in the centre of each square. Close to make a pastry envelope by folding in the four corners towards the centre. Pinch along the edges of the pastry and pinch together in the centre. Turn on the oven to 375°F/190°C/Gas 5. Beat the second egg and brush each envelope with egg. Put on greased baking trays and sprinkle with sesame seeds. Bake in the oven until the pies turn golden (25–35 minutes). Makes 16–20 pies.

Spinach Triangles (*Spanakotrígona*)

1½ lb (675 g) spinach
3 tablespoons olive oil
1 onion, finely chopped
6 spring onions, sliced
1 cup crumbled feta cheese

2 tablespoons chopped parsley *or* coriander leaf
1 teaspoon marjoram *or* oregano
1 lb (450 g) fillo pastry
clarified butter *or* olive oil

Wash the spinach and chop. Heat the oil in a pan and gently fry the onion and spring onions until they soften. Add the spinach and cook for 2 minutes. Stir well so that the spinach is well covered with oil. Mix in the cheese and green herbs. Do not add salt because feta is salted already.

Cut the fillo sheets lengthwise into strips 4–5 inches (10–12 cm) wide. Put on a pastry board and brush with melted butter or oil. Put a little of the filling at one end of a strip and fold up in triangular fashion like a flag. To do this imagine a square at one end of the strip. Divide this into 2 triangles. Put some filling on the second triangle and fold the first triangle across it. Carry on folding up the triangular packet until you reach the end of the strip. Put the stuffed triangles on greased baking sheets and bake in the oven at 375°F/190°C/Gas 5 until crisp and golden (15–25 minutes).

Stuffed Tomatoes (*Domátes Yemistés*)

8 large tomatoes
½ cup olive oil
1 onion, finely chopped
4 cloves garlic, finely chopped
2 cups cooked rice
1 cup chopped walnuts *or* almonds

1 cup breadcrumbs
2 teaspoons salt
½ teaspoon freshly ground pepper
2 teaspoons basil *or* oregano
2 tablespoons chopped parsley *or* coriander leaf

Wash the tomatoes and slice off and keep the tops. Scoop out the pulp and keep. Arrange the tomatoes on a greased baking dish. Heat the oil in a pan and gently fry the onion for 2 minutes. Add the garlic, rice, nuts, breadcrumbs and tomato pulp. Sprinkle with salt, pepper, basil and chopped herb. Mix together and fry for 3 minutes. Put some of the filling in each tomato and put the tops back on. Bake in the oven at 375°F/190°C/Gas 5 for 30 minutes.

Baked Vegetables with Sesame Sauce (*Láhana sto Fúrno me Tahíni*)

2 lb (900 g) mixed vegetables
1 onion, chopped
2 tablespoons chopped parsley *or*
  coriander leaf
2 teaspoons salt
½ teaspoon pepper

2 teaspoons marjoram *or* oregano
4 tablespoons olive oil
1 cup sesame paste
juice of 1 lemon
2–4 cloves garlic, finely chopped

Wash and trim the vegetables and cut in small pieces. Mix in the onion and parsley and put in a casserole or ovenproof dish. Sprinkle with the seasoning and olive oil. Stir the sesame paste, lemon juice and garlic together in a bowl. Add a little water until a creamy consistency is obtained. Add to the vegetables. Bake in the oven at 375°F/190°C/Gas 5 for 30 minutes. Serve with a salad.

Vegetable Stew (*Láhana Yahní*)

½ cup olive oil
1 onion, chopped
1 aubergine, cut in cubes
4 courgettes, sliced
2 sticks celery, sliced
4 tomatoes, chopped

2 tablespoons chopped parsley *or*
  coriander leaf
2–4 cloves garlic, finely chopped
1 teaspoon salt
½ teaspoon freshly ground pepper
2 cups water *or* stock

Heat the oil in a pan and gently fry the onion for 2 minutes. Add the aubergine and cook for 2 minutes. Add the courgettes, celery, tomatoes, herb and garlic. Stir together. Sprinkle on the salt and pepper. Simmer for 2 minutes more then add 2 cups of water or stock. Cook until the vegetables are tender.

Vegetable Fritters (*Láhana Tiganitá*)

For the batter:
1 cup flour
1 teaspoon salt
pinch of freshly ground pepper
¾–1 cup warm water
1 egg, beaten
1 tablespoon olive oil

For the fritters:
2 large potatoes
1 aubergine, sliced
4 courgettes, sliced
2 firm tomatoes, sliced
1 green pepper, seeded and sliced
olive oil for deep-frying

Make up the batter by sifting the flour with the salt and pepper. Make a well in the middle and add the water, stirring in gradually to make a smooth mixture. Mix in the egg and olive oil. The mixture should make a creamy batter. Leave to stand while you prepare the vegetables. Stir well just before use.

Boil the potato until almost soft and slice. Meanwhile prepare the rest of the vegetables. Heat some oil in a deep-frying pan and fry the vegetable slices after dipping them in the batter. When they are golden, remove and allow to drain on absorbent paper. Serve with a selection of sauces (see Sauces pp. 128–32).

Vegetable Moussaka (*Láhana Musaká*)

2 aubergines
olive oil for frying
2 onions, chopped
4 tomatoes, chopped
2–4 cloves garlic, finely chopped
½ lb (225 g) mushrooms, sliced
½ lb (225 g) carrots, sliced
1 lb (450 g) potatoes, sliced
2 teaspoons salt

½ teaspoon freshly ground pepper
2 small pieces cinnamon
3 tablespoons clarified butter *or*
  margarine
3 tablespoons flour
1½ pints (900 ml) milk
½ teaspoon freshly grated nutmeg
6 allspice berries

Trim and slice the aubergines. Heat a cup of oil in a frying pan and lightly fry the aubergine slices. Remove and drain on absorbent paper. Add more oil if necessary and gently fry the onion for 2 minutes. Add the tomatoes, garlic and other vegetables. Sprinkle with the salt, pepper and cinnamon and fry together for 3 minutes. Now make the white sauce. In a small saucepan gently heat the butter. Gradually stir in the flour, then the milk. Add a pinch of salt and pepper and the nutmeg and simmer gently for 1 minute.

Grease the sides and base of a casserole or baking dish and put in a layer of aubergine slices. Spoon on a layer of fried vegetables. Do this until the dish is nearly full then cover with the white sauce. Push the allspice berries into the sauce and bake in the oven at 375°F/190°C/Gas 5 until the top is golden (about 30 minutes).

Hard cheese could be added to this dish. Grate ½ lb (225 g) cheese and sprinkle over the fried vegetables adding a layer of white sauce on top.

Moussakas can be made with various fillings so that you can invent your own. A true moussaka must have a topping of white sauce and it must include aubergines in the ingredients. Try layers of fried nuts and dried fruit, chestnuts and cooked mashed chick peas. Use other herbs and spices.

Pikilia

Pikilía means a variety or assortment. A meal is made up by putting small portions of various dishes on one plate. If you have guests you could put all the dishes on the table and let each person make up his own pikilia. A possible assortment could be: cucumber and yogurt dip (*dzadzíki*), omelette, fried potatoes, sliced tomatoes, sliced onion, chopped parsley leaf, chick pea patties, aubergine fritters, sliced green beans.

The ideal pikilia would be balanced nutritionally as well as having an attractive appearance.

Salads (*Salátes*)

The salad is a favourite way for Greeks to eat vegetables. As the first of the spring vegetables appear, simple salads are made of raw greens and lettuce with spring onions, radishes, cheese and olives, dressed with olive oil and lemon juice or wine vinegar. Greeks like to boil immature greens for use in salads. Stalks of wild thistle (which is somewhat like an artichoke) are boiled and dressed with garlic sauce after the spiky leaves have been stripped off. Many plants are used in this way before they flower.

Apple Salad (*Mílo Saláta*)

3 apples, cored and chopped
1 onion, cut in rings
4 tablespoons yogurt
pinch of freshly ground pepper

juice of 1 lemon
crumbled feta cheese
1 tablespoon chopped parsley *or*
    coriander leaf

Combine the apples, onion, yogurt, pepper and lemon juice. Sprinkle with cheese and serve garnished with chopped herb.

Apple and Chestnut Salad
(*Mílo ke Kástano Saláta*)

2 apples, cored and chopped
3 sticks celery, sliced
3 tablespoons chopped cooked
  chestnuts

4 tablespoons olive oil
2 tablespoons wine vinegar
crumbled feta cheese
1 teaspoon marjoram *or* oregano

Combine the apples, celery and chestnuts with the oil and vinegar.
Sprinkle with the cheese. Garnish with dried herb.

Artichoke Salad
(*Anginára Saláta*)

4 small globe artichokes
4 tomatoes
2–4 cloves garlic, finely chopped
2 tablespoons olive oil

1 teaspoon marjoram *or* oregano
2 teaspoons chopped mint leaf
salt to taste
lemon

Prepare the artichokes by cutting any stalk to about 1 inch (2 cm).
Trim off any tough outer leaves with spines. Trim off the top and
remove any hairy choke. Keep any succulent leaves which can be
eaten. Cut the stalk lengthwise into 2 or 4 pieces. Cut the rest of the
artichoke in small pieces. Make up a tomato sauce by chopping the
tomatoes in small pieces. Mix together with the garlic, oil, herbs and
salt. Stir the artichoke pieces into the fresh tomato mixture and serve
with wedges of lemon.

Beetroot Salad (*Kokkinoyúli Saláta*)

Beetroots were popular in ancient Greece, but they are not seen as
much today. This recipe can be made when the beetroots are just
cooked or when they have been allowed to cool.

1 lb (450 g) beetroots
oil and vinegar sauce (see p. 130)
1 small onion, cut in rings

1 tablespoon chopped parsley *or*
  dill leaf

Wash the beetroots and boil in slightly salted water until tender. Peel
and slice. Add the oil and vinegar dressing. Decorate with onion and
chopped herb.

Cabbage Salad (*Láhano Saláta*)

½ firm white cabbage
4 tablespoons olive oil
3 tablespoons lemon juice

pinch of salt
pinch of freshly ground pepper
1 small onion, finely sliced

Wash the cabbage and discard the wilted outer leaves. Slice the firm part of the cabbage finely and toss with the oil and lemon, salt and pepper. Mix in the fresh onion slices.

Cabbage and Carrot Salad (*Láhano ke Karóto Saláta*)

10 oz (280 g) firm white cabbage, sliced
10 oz (280 g) carrot, finely sliced *or* grated
1 onion, finely chopped
1 teaspoon sunflower seeds

1 teaspoon sesame seeds
4 tablespoons olive oil
2 tablespoons wine vinegar
½ teaspoon salt
pinch of freshly ground pepper

Combine all the ingredients and mix well.

Cabbage and Egg Salad (*Láhano ke Avgó Saláta*)

10 oz (280 g) firm white cabbage, sliced
4 tomatoes, sliced
2 carrots, sliced
4 hard-boiled eggs, sliced

2 apples, cored and chopped
2 tablespoons olive oil
½ teaspoon salt
pinch of freshly ground pepper
black olives

Combine the cabbage with the tomatoes, carrots, egg and apple. Pour the oil over the salad and sprinkle on salt and pepper. Garnish with olives.

Carrot Salad (*Karotosaláta*)

Use 1 carrot and 1 teaspoon sunflower seeds per person. Slice the carrot and mix with the sunflower seeds. Cover with oil and lemon sauce (see p. 130) and decorate with black olives.

Cauliflower Salad (*Kunupídhi Saláta*)

1 cauliflower
1 teaspoon salt
oil and lemon sauce (see p. 130)

Wash and trim the cauliflower and cut into florets. Boil in salted water until tender. Drain. Add the oil and lemon sauce.
  Broccoli may be treated the same way.

Celery Salad (*Sélinosaláta*)

4 sticks celery, sliced
2 apples, cored and chopped
½ cup sliced blanched almonds *or*
  chopped walnuts
2 tablespoons wine vinegar
3 tablespoons olive oil
1 tablespoon sesame seeds
½ teaspoon salt

Mix the celery, apple and nuts in a bowl. Add the vinegar and olive oil. Sprinkle with sesame seeds and salt.

Chestnut Salad (*Kástano Saláta*)

1 lb (450 g) roasted *or* boiled
  chestnuts
1 tablespoon finely chopped onion
1 tablespoon chopped parsley *or*
  coriander leaf
1 teaspoon chopped sage leaf
1 teaspoon salt
½ teaspoon freshly ground pepper
1 cup yogurt *or* soft cheese

Pound or slice the chestnuts. Mix together with the rest of the ingredients and serve with fresh lettuce leaves and lemon wedges.

Country Salad (*Saláta Horiátiki*)

Known as the mixed salad of the country and village people, this salad is the most popular with city people and tourists. The contents will vary according to season, but it should include some green vegetable, olives and feta cheese sprinkled with herbs. One person will need a salad containing:

a few radishes
2 tomatoes, chopped
a few slices cucumber
a few crisp lettuce leaves, sliced
½ green pepper, sliced
1 spring onion, sliced
1 tablespoon chopped parsley *or*
    coriander leaf

2 tablespoons olive oil
1 tablespoon wine vinegar
pinch of salt
pinch of freshly ground pepper
4 oz (100 g) feta cheese, crumbled
    or sliced
a few black olives
1 teaspoon marjoram *or* oregano

Mix the salad vegetables together in a bowl and pour over the oil and vinegar. Sprinkle on salt, pepper and cheese. Put in a few olives and sprinkle the cheese with the marjoram or oregano.

Courgette Salad (*Kolokithákia Vrastá Saláta*)

4 courgettes
salt
1 tablespoon olive oil

1 tablespoon lemon juice
pinch of freshly ground pepper
pinch of dried herbs

Wash and trim the courgettes. Boil until just tender in slightly salted water. Slice into thick rounds. Add the oil and lemon and sprinkle with salt, pepper and dried herbs.

This simple preparation can be used with a variety of vegetables such as cauliflower, spinach, beetroot, young dandelion leaves or other wild greens.

Courgette and Onion Salad (*Kolokithákia ke Krommídhi Saláta*)

1 lb (450 g) courgettes
1 small onion, cut in rings
½ green pepper, sliced
1 tablespoon chopped parsley
1 teaspoon marjoram *or* oregano

2 tablespoons olive oil
1 tablespoon wine vinegar
½ teaspoon salt
pinch of freshly ground pepper
black olives

Trim, slice and cook the courgettes in boiling salted water until they are tender (a few minutes). Drain and put in a salad bowl. Mix in the rest of the ingredients. Serve with lettuce or a green salad and cheese.

Cucumber Salad (*Angúrosalata*)

½ cucumber, sliced
1 small green pepper, cored and
  sliced
2 tomatoes, chopped
pinch of salt
pinch of freshly ground pepper

1 tablespoon olive oil
1 tablespoon lemon juice *or* wine
  vinegar
1 tablespoon chopped mint leaf *or*
  parsley
a few black olives

Mix the cucumber, green pepper and tomato. Sprinkle with seasoning
and add the oil and lemon juice. Garnish with chopped herb and
olives.

Cucumber and Grape Salad
(*Angúri ke Stafíli Saláta*)

½ cucumber, sliced
1 cup seedless grapes
2 tablespoons chopped parsley
1 cup yogurt

½ teaspoon salt
pinch of freshly ground pepper
1 teaspoon marjoram *or* oregano

Mix the cucumber with the grapes and chopped herb. Stir in the
yogurt and sprinkle with the seasoning.

Cucumber and Yogurt Salad
(*Angúri ke Yaúrti Saláta*)

½ cucumber, sliced
2 cloves garlic, finely chopped
2 teaspoons chopped mint leaf

1 cup yogurt
½ teaspoon salt
pinch of freshly ground pepper

Mix the cucumber, garlic, mint and yogurt. Sprinkle with salt and
pepper.

Dandelion Salad (*Radhíkosalata*)

1 bunch young dandelion leaves,
  chopped
1 bunch wild green herbs, chopped
2 tablespoons olive oil
1 tablespoon wine vinegar *or*
  lemon juice

pinch of salt
pinch of freshly ground pepper
2 radishes, sliced
2 tomatoes, chopped

Wash the green leaves. Mix the oil and vinegar with the salt and pepper and add to the greens. Garnish with radish and tomato.

Any other edible wild green herbs such as chicory, hawkbit or wintergreen may be added to this salad and the quantities may be varied according to taste.

Dandelion and Lettuce Salad (*Radhíki ke Marúli Saláta*)

½ lettuce, washed and shredded
1 cup dandelion leaves, washed and shredded
a few fresh mint leaves
a few radishes, sliced

1 onion, finely chopped
½ cup crumbled feta cheese
1 teaspoon salt
pinch of freshly ground pepper

Mix the ingredients together and serve with oil and lemon sauce (see p. 130).

Grape Salad (*Stafíli Saláta*)

8 oz (225 g) grapes
a few lettuce leaves, shredded
2 sticks celery, sliced
2 tomatoes, chopped
2 tablespoons chopped walnuts

4 tablespoons olive oil
2 tablespoons wine vinegar
½ teaspoon salt
crumbled feta cheese

Cut the grapes in half and remove the pips. Combine with the rest of the ingredients except the cheese. Sprinkle on a little cheese. Cottage cheese or curd cheese may be substituted for the feta. You may then need a little more salt in the seasoning.

Green Salad (*Saláta Prásina*)

1 bunch dandelion leaves, chopped
a few lettuce leaves, shredded
a few cabbage leaves, shredded
½ green pepper, sliced
fresh carrot tops, sliced
fresh radish tops, sliced
a few spring onions, sliced
3 tablespoons olive oil

1 tablespoon wine vinegar
pinch of salt
pinch of freshly ground pepper
½ teaspoon marjoram, oregano *or* basil
1 tablespoon chopped parsley *or* coriander leaf

Wash and prepare the vegetables. Make the dressing by beating the oil, vinegar, salt, pepper and dried herb together. Mix well with the green salad. Sprinkle with the chopped fresh herb.

Colour contrast could be added with black olives, tomatoes or sliced radish.

Green Bean Salad (*Fasolákia Saláta*)

1 lb (450 g) green *or* French beans
2 tablespoons olive oil

1 tablespoon lemon juice *or* wine vinegar

Trim and slice the beans and cook in a little boiling salted water until just tender. Drain and leave to cool. Add the oil and lemon juice.

Green Pepper Salad (*Piperiá Saláta*)

2 green peppers, cored and sliced
4 tomatoes, chopped
1 cup black olives
½ cup chopped walnuts, hazel nuts *or* blanched almonds

1 teaspoon salt
pinch of freshly ground pepper
3 tablespoons olive oil
1 tablespoon lemon juice

Combine the peppers, tomatoes, olives and nuts. Sprinkle with seasoning and add the oil and lemon juice.

Leek Salad (*Prásosalata*)

1 lb (450 g) leeks
½ cup black olives
4 tomatoes, chopped

2 tablespoons olive oil
1 tablespoon wine vinegar

Wash and trim the leeks. Slice and boil in slightly salted water until just tender. Drain and add the rest of the ingredients.

Lettuce Salad (*Marúli Saláta*)

In the winter, cabbage, cauliflower and broccoli are at their cheapest and best and they are served daily as a salad. After these greens comes the cos lettuce, said to have been developed on the Dodecanese island of Kos. This long-leaved crisp variety of lettuce is known as *marúli*, while other varieties come under the collective term of *saláta*. When you buy a large lettuce in Greece it is customary to be given a big green onion or bunch of spring onions with it. This, of course, is essential to the lettuce salad.

1 lettuce
a few spring onions, sliced
3 tablespoons olive oil
1 tablespoon wine vinegar
½ teaspoon salt

pinch of freshly ground pepper
½ teaspoon basil, marjoram *or* oregano
½ teaspoon finely chopped garlic

Wash the lettuce and separate the leaves. Allow to drain. Beat the rest of the ingredients in a bowl. Add the lettuce leaves and turn them gently so that all the leaves become coated with the dressing.

Lettuce, Radish and Cheese Salad (*Marúli me Repanáki ke Tirí Saláta*)

1 lettuce
1 bunch radishes
a few spring onions, sliced
½ cup crumbled feta cheese
juice of 1 lemon

½ teaspoon freshly ground pepper
3 tablespoons olive oil
1 tablespoon chopped parsley *or* coriander leaf

Wash and chop the lettuce and allow to drain. Mix the lettuce, radishes and spring onion in a salad bowl. Sprinkle with the rest of the ingredients and turn the salad so the lettuce is well coated with oil.

Melon Salad (*Pepóni Saláta*)

1 melon
2–3 tomatoes, chopped
1 cup black olives
2 tablespoons lemon juice

4 tablespoons olive oil
1 tablespoon clear honey
pinch of salt
a few mint leaves, chopped

Slice the melon in half. Cut out the melon flesh and discard the skin and seeds. Cut the melon in small pieces. Mix in a bowl with the tomatoes and olives. Make a dressing by mixing the lemon juice, oil, honey and salt and pour it over the melon mixture. Garnish with the chopped mint leaf. Serve with beans and yogurt.

Mountain Herbs Salad (*Hórta Vunó Saláta*)

This salad made with herbs found on mountain slopes is delicious with hard-boiled eggs. The herbs can either be eaten fresh or gently boiled and served with olive oil, lemon juice and some cheese and olives. Suggested herbs which can be mixed according to your own preference are: borage, mint, marjoram, dandelion, mallow, coriander, parsley, dill.

Mushroom Salad (*Manitári Saláta*)

2 tablespoons olive oil
8 oz (225 g) mushrooms, sliced
2 cloves garlic, finely chopped
1 teaspoon basil *or* thyme
2 tablespoons lemon juice
½ cup water

1 tomato, chopped
1 teaspoon salt
pinch of freshly ground pepper
1 tablespoon chopped parsley *or*
 coriander leaf

Heat the oil in a pan and gently fry the mushrooms for 2 minutes. Add the garlic and basil and mix well with the oil. Fry for a further minute. Add the lemon juice, ½ cup water, tomato, salt and pepper and mix well. Cook on a low heat until the tomato begins to soften. Remove from the heat and allow to cool. Serve garnished with the chopped herb.

A simple mushroom salad can be made without any cooking. Slice the mushrooms, squeeze on lemon juice and sprinkle with a little fresh pepper and chopped or dried herbs to taste.

Mushroom and Yogurt Salad
(*Manitári ke Yaúrti Saláta*)

2 tablespoons olive oil
8 oz (225 g) mushrooms, sliced
½ teaspoon thyme *or* other dried
 herb
½ cup water
1 teaspoon salt

1 cup yogurt
1–2 cloves garlic, finely chopped
1 tablespoon chopped parsley *or*
 coriander leaf
lemon juice

Heat the oil in a pan and gently fry the mushrooms for 2 minutes. Add the herb and mix well. Add ½ cup water and cook for 2 minutes more. Remove from the heat. Stir the salt into the yogurt and add to the mushrooms. Mix gently and sprinkle with garlic, chopped fresh herb and a little lemon juice.

Olive Salad (*Eliá Saláta*)

2 cups black olives
½ cup chopped walnuts *or* blanched almonds
1 small onion, cut in rings
2 tomatoes, chopped

½ green pepper, sliced
1 tablespoon chopped parsley *or* coriander leaf
4 tablespoons olive oil
2 tablespoons lemon juice

Mix the olives, nuts, onion, tomato, green pepper and parsley together. Sprinkle with oil and lemon juice. Serve with bread and lettuce.

Olive and Orange Salad (*Eliá ke Portokáli Saláta*)

2 cups black olives
2 oranges, peeled and cut in pieces
1 small onion, cut in rings
½ cup sliced beetroot
½ cup sliced celery

2 tablespoons olive oil
1 tablespoon lemon juice
pinch of salt
pinch of freshly ground pepper
pinch of marjoram *or* oregano

Mix together the olives, orange, onion, beetroot and celery. Add the oil and lemon juice. Sprinkle with seasoning and mix well.

Potato Salad (*Patáta Saláta*)

2 lb (900 g) potatoes
1 onion, finely sliced
1–2 cloves garlic, finely chopped
1 tablespoon chopped parsley *or* coriander leaf

4 tablespoons olive oil
2 tablespoons wine vinegar
1 teaspoon salt
½ teaspoon freshly ground pepper

Clean the potatoes and boil in slightly salted water until tender but not mushy. When cool, remove the skins if desired and cut in small cubes. Sprinkle with the onion and the rest of the ingredients. Mix well.

Potato and Beetroot Salad (*Patáta ke Kokkinoyúli Saláta*)

1 lb (450 g) potatoes
1 cup sliced cooked beetroot
½ cup thickly sliced cucumber
2 spring onions, *or* a few chives, chopped
1 cup yogurt

1 teaspoon salt
½ teaspoon freshly ground pepper
½ cup olive oil
1 tablespoon chopped parsley *or* coriander leaf

Clean the potatoes and boil in slightly salted water until tender. Peel if the skin is very thick. Allow to cool. Chop the beetroot and cucumber slices. Cut the potato in small cubes. Gently stir the yogurt with the potato. Add the beetroot, cucumber and onion. Sprinkle with salt and pepper. Gradually mix in the oil and serve garnished with the green herb.

Potato and Egg Salad
(*Patáta ke Avgó Saláta*)

1 lb (450 g) potatoes
4 hard-boiled eggs
2 tablespoons chopped parsley *or*
  coriander leaf

1 teaspoon salt
½ teaspoon freshly ground pepper
4 tablespoons olive oil
2 tablespoons wine vinegar

Clean the potatoes and boil in slightly salted water until tender. Peel if the skins are very thick. Cut in small pieces. Slice the eggs. Mix the potato and egg gently. Sprinkle with the seasoning and pour the oil and vinegar over. Mix together.

Potato and Sesame Salad
(*Patáta ke Tahíni Saláta*)

1 lb (450 g) potatoes
½–1 cup sesame paste
juice of 1 lemon
1 teaspoon salt
½ teaspoon freshly ground pepper

2 tablespoons olive oil
1 small onion, cut in rings
a few black olives
1 tablespoon chopped parsley *or*
  coriander leaf

Boil the potatoes in slightly salted water until tender. Peel if the skins are very thick. Mash. Stir in the sesame paste to taste. Add the lemon juice. Sprinkle with salt and pepper and mix well. Spread out the mixture on a serving dish and add a little oil. Decorate with onion, olives and green herb.

Potato and Yogurt Salad
(*Patáta ke Yaúrti Saláta*)

2 lb (900 g) potatoes
2 cups yogurt
1–2 teaspoons salt
½ teaspoon freshly ground pepper
2 teaspoons marjoram *or* oregano

2–4 spring onions, sliced
2–4 cloves garlic, finely chopped
4 tablespoons olive oil
a few black olives
a few lettuce leaves

Boil the potatoes in slightly salted water until they are tender. Peel and mash. Stir in the yogurt. Season with salt, pepper and herb. Sprinkle with the onion and garlic. Stir in the oil until a thick creamy consistency is reached. Decorate with olives and lettuce leaves. Serve with pitta bread or toasted slices of bread.

This salad is delicious with slices of cucumber, tomato or cooked beetroot. Sprinkle with lemon juice or wine vinegar as desired.

Red Bean Salad (*Fasóli Saláta*)

3 cups cooked red kidney beans
1 onion, finely sliced
2 sticks celery, sliced
1 teaspoon salt
½ teaspoon freshly ground pepper

4 tablespoons olive oil
2 tablespoons wine vinegar
1 tablespoon chopped parsley *or* coriander leaf

Put the beans in a salad bowl and mix with the rest of the ingredients.

Red Bean and Apple Salad (*Fasóli ke Mílo Saláta*)

2 cups cooked red kidney beans
1 onion, finely sliced
2 apples, cored and chopped
1 tablespoon chopped parsley *or* coriander leaf
1 teaspoon salt
pinch of freshly ground pepper

½ teaspoon mustard
1 teaspoon basil, marjoram *or* oregano
2–4 cloves garlic, finely chopped
2 tablespoons olive oil
1 tablespoon wine vinegar

Put the beans in a salad bowl and combine with the rest of the ingredients. The quantities may be adjusted to suit your taste.

Tomato Salad (*Domátosalata*)

4 tomatoes, chopped
½ onion, finely sliced
1 teaspoon salt
pinch of freshly ground pepper
½ teaspoon basil

½ teaspoon marjoram *or* oregano
3 tablespoons olive oil
2 tablespoons wine vinegar
1 tablespoon chopped mint leaf
a few black olives

Mix the tomatoes and onion. Sprinkle on the seasoning and add the oil and vinegar. Decorate with olives and mint leaf.

A simple tomato salad can be made by cutting up some tomatoes. Sprinkle a little ground aniseed over them with salt and pepper. Mix with oil and vinegar.

Tomato and Cucumber Salad
(*Angurodomáta Saláta*)

8 oz (225 g) tomatoes, chopped
8 oz (225 g) cucumber, cut in thick
  slices
2 spring onions, sliced
1–2 cloves garlic, finely chopped

2 teaspoons basil
½ teaspoon ground aniseed
1 teaspoon salt
1 tablespoon chopped dill leaf *or*
  coriander leaf

Mix the tomatoes, cucumber and onion together. Sprinkle with the garlic, basil and seasoning. Mix together and garnish with chopped green herb. Serve with oil and vinegar sauce (see p. 130) or with yogurt and bread.

Tomato and Green Pepper Salad
(*Domáta ke Piperiá Saláta*)

8 oz (225 g) tomatoes, chopped
8 oz (225 g) green pepper, cored
  and sliced
1 small onion, finely chopped
½ cup crumbled feta cheese
a few black olives

1 tablespoon chopped parsley *or*
  coriander leaf
1 teaspoon marjoram *or* oregano
½ teaspoon salt
pinch of freshly ground pepper
3 tablespoons olive oil
2 tablespoons wine vinegar

Mix the tomatoes, pepper, onion and cheese with the olives. Sprinkle with the chopped herb, salt and pepper. Mix together and add the oil and vinegar.

Tomato and Breadcrumbs Salad
(*Domatósalata me Psíhula*)

1 cup breadcrumbs
4 tomatoes, chopped
1 onion, finely chopped
1–2 cloves garlic, finely chopped
1 tablespoon chopped parsley *or*
  coriander leaf

a few mint, basil *or* other herb
  leaves, chopped
1 teaspoon salt
pinch of freshly ground pepper
juice of 1 lemon
1–2 tablespoons olive oil

Put the breadcrumbs under the grill or heat gently in a frying pan for a few minutes. Put in a salad dish. Add the tomatoes, onion, garlic, herbs, salt and pepper. Mix together well. Sprinkle with the lemon juice and olive oil. Wine vinegar may be substituted for the lemon juice, and crushed cereals, such as oats or wheat, may be substituted for the breadcrumbs. Serve with yogurt and beans.

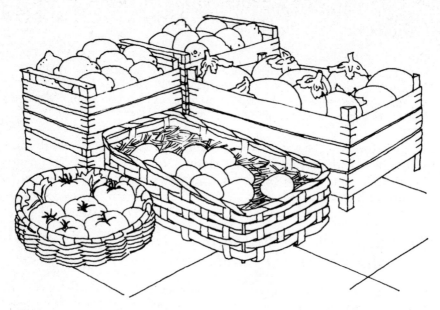

Eggs (*Avgá*)

Baked Vegetable Omelette (*Sfungáto*)

The Greeks have their own word for omelette though the international word *omelétta* is also widespread. The word *omelette* has reached English via the French via the Latin word for a flat layer – *lamella*. It is highly probable that the ancient Greeks taught the Romans how to make omelettes. Here is a baked omelette popular in the Dodecanese.

½ cup olive oil
2 onions, chopped
2–4 cloves garlic, finely chopped
1 cup sliced mushrooms
1 cup sliced courgettes
½ cup crumbled feta cheese
2 tablespoons chopped parsley *or*
    coriander leaf

2 teaspoons salt
½ teaspoon freshly ground pepper
1 cup water
8 eggs, beaten
breadcrumbs

Heat the oil in a pan and gently fry the onion for 2 minutes. Add the garlic, mushrooms and courgettes and fry for a further 2 minutes. Add the cheese, chopped herb, salt, pepper and a cup of water. Mix together and add the eggs. Grease a baking dish and sprinkle with breadcrumbs. Pour in the omelette mixture and bake in the oven at 375°F/190°C/Gas 5 until the top is golden (25–30 minutes). Serve with a salad.

Courgette Omelette (*Omelétta me Kolokithákia*)

2 tablespoons olive oil
2 courgettes, sliced
pinch of salt
pinch of freshly ground pepper

pinch of marjoram *or* oregano
3 eggs, beaten
1 tablespoon chopped parsley *or* coriander leaf

Heat the oil in a frying pan and fry the courgettes until tender. Sprinkle with the seasoning and stir in the eggs. Keep stirring towards the centre of the pan until the egg sets. Allow to cook then turn the omelette over and cook on the other side. If the omelette threatens to break, put a plate on top of the pan and turn the omelette on to the plate. Slide the omelette back into the pan to cook on the other side. Sprinkle with the chopped herb and serve with a salad.

Onion Omelette (*Omelétta me Krommídhi*)

4 eggs
1 tablespoon chopped parsley *or* coriander leaf
1 onion, finely chopped
2 cloves garlic, finely chopped

½ teaspoon salt
pinch of freshly ground pepper
pinch of dried herbs
2 tablespoons olive oil

Beat the eggs well. Stir in the rest of the ingredients except the oil. Heat the oil in a pan and gently fry the egg mixture. Turn and allow to cook for 1–2 minutes on the other side. Serve with a salad.

Potato Omelette (*Omelétta me Patátes*)

1 lb (450 g) peeled potatoes
2 tablespoons olive oil
1 teaspoon salt
pinch of freshly ground pepper
4 eggs, beaten

1 tablespoon chopped parsley *or* coriander leaf
lemon
cucumber

Boil the potatoes until tender. Slice or cut in small cubes. Heat the oil in a frying pan and add the potato. Sprinkle with salt and pepper. Allow to fry until the potato begins to turn golden. Pour the eggs over and stir together until the eggs begin to set. Turn and allow to cook on the other side. Sprinkle with chopped herbs and serve with slices of lemon and cucumber.

The same technique can be used with chopped tomato, courgettes or aubergines. These may also be mixed up to make a tasty omelette.

Spinach Omelette (*Omelétta me Spanáki*)

8 oz (225 g) spinach
4 eggs
3 tablespoons olive oil

½ teaspoon salt
pinch of freshly ground pepper
pinch of ground aniseed

Wash the spinach and chop finely. Beat the eggs well. Heat a tablespoon of oil in a large pan and fry the spinach gently for 3 minutes. Sprinkle with the seasoning. In another pan heat the remaining oil and pour in the eggs. As the omelette begins to set, put the fried spinach in the soft centre. Cook for another minute and turn the omelette to cook on the other side. Serve with a salad or potatoes.

Tomato Omelette (*Omelétta me Domátes*)

4 tablespoons olive oil
2 spring onions, sliced
4 tomatoes, chopped
2 cloves garlic, finely chopped
1 teaspoon salt

pinch of freshly ground pepper
1 teaspoon basil
4 eggs, beaten
1 tablespoon chopped parsley *or* coriander leaf

Heat the oil in a pan and gently fry the onion until it softens. Add the tomatoes and garlic. Sprinkle with salt, pepper and basil. Fry together for 2 minutes. Add the eggs and cook until the egg sets. Turn and cook on the other side. Serve garnished with chopped herb.

Vegetable Omelette (*Omelétta me Lahaniká*)

1 lb (450 g) courgettes, trimmed
  and sliced
½ cup shelled broad beans
4 tablespoons olive oil

6 eggs, beaten
1 teaspoon chopped mint leaf
1 teaspoon salt
½ teaspoon freshly ground pepper

Put the courgettes and beans in a frying pan and add the oil. Heat gently and add the eggs. Sprinkle with the seasoning, stir and cook until the egg sets. Turn and allow to cook on the other side. Serve hot or cold with a salad.

Scrambled Eggs (*Avgá Sfungáto*)

1 tablespoon clarified butter *or*
  olive oil
6 eggs
½ teaspoon salt

pinch of freshly ground pepper
pinch of chopped *or* dried herbs
crumbled feta cheese

Put a frying pan on a low heat and add the butter. Break in the eggs and sprinkle with salt, pepper and herbs to taste. Stir the mixture until the eggs solidify. Place on a serving dish just before the egg dries up. Sprinkle with cheese and serve either on its own, with bread or with a salad.

Easter Eggs

Eggs are a popular everyday food in Greece, especially in the form of an omelette. At Eastertime, however, the egg (*avgó*) becomes an important symbol of rebirth and creative joy.

The Easter egg should be hard-boiled, plunged in cold water and dried. Die each egg a deep carmine red. Drain, allow to dry and then wipe with a cloth dipped in olive oil to give the egg a gloss. Give the egg a final wipe with a dry cloth to shine.

After the Easter soup has been tasted, just after midnight on Easter Saturday, you are ready to play the Easter egg game (*Tsúngrizma*). One person holds an egg out while the other taps it with his egg from above. If your egg cracks you lose. The winner goes on to have the first tap at the next egg. One consolation for the loser is that he can now eat his egg with a nice piece of *tsuréki*!

Mizithra!

Mihail owned a little white house with a vegetable patch and a grove of oranges and lemons. Nearby he had some fields and vineyards which he worked until mid-afternoon. In the evening we would sit on his balcony and discuss the state of the vegetables, the fate of priests at Eastertime, the misfortune of having to work in Athens – using a variety of languages, gestures and mime. The subject of cheese came up and Mihail was quick to grasp that, although I knew the names of many cheeses, I had only experienced *féta*. He regarded me for a moment with a look of pity, then jumped up.

'Come on, we're going for a walk.'

As we made a quick tour of the village, Mihail pointed into the dark sky and spoke the names of the stars, as if he was composing a poem for the occasion.

'They're nothing,' he waved his hand scornfully. 'You wait.'

We stepped into a taverna run by Mihail's friend, Yoryos. Mihail ordered some bread and some bottles of retsina – and *mizíthra*. Yoryos moved his head downwards and let out a sigh. He whispered '*mizíthra*' and smiled. Mihail rolled his eyes and made as if to swoon when the word was mentioned again. Was it a word for some beautiful woman, I wondered.

The bread and wine arrived, along with a plate on which there was a large slab of white cheese. Mihail lunged at it with a fork then sat back to watch me as I tasted it. Yes, he was right – it was rich and creamy; it was velvety; it had the quality of a starlit sky; it was delicious. Mihail slapped me on the back and laughed.

'He likes it!' he shouted and ordered another portion. My feeble protests were refused. I managed to eat half of the second slab before I began to feel queasy. Perhaps another glass of retsina would help. Then I had a brainwave. In the corner a party of Germans had just finished their meal. I went over to them with the plate of cheese.

'Try it,' I said. '*Mizíthra*, it's delicious!'

'Ya?' they nodded and tucked in. Relieved, I sat down again. A moment later a further plate of cheese appeared on the table.

'The Germans like it. They have ordered some to take home,' Yoryos whispered. 'This is a thank you from me.'

Mihail grinned and refused to help me eat the cheese. I must have the honour. With the aid of more retsina I forced it down.

'You really like it,' said Mihail. I thought I could detect admiration in his voice. Then Yoryos was at the table with a fourth helping of *mizíthra*.

'From your German friends,' he crooned. I turned round. Four red faces beamed at me.

'Ya – iss for you!'

'*Danke schön,*' I croaked.

Yoryos sat down on a chair between us. '*Mizíthra,*' he sighed, his body swaying with emotion. 'My wife makes it, every piece, with her own hands.'

Mihail filled our glasses, crashed his own against the bottle and lifted it high. '*Mizíthra,*' he shouted.

The Germans pushed back their chairs. '*Mizíthra!*' they cried.

Cheese (*Tirí*)

Traditionally, Greek cheeses are made from goat's or sheep's milk and cow's milk is still largely imported. Here is a list of cheeses which are generally available:

Féta: Probably the best known and most popular Greek cheese. It is a soft white cheese, made from goat's or sheep's milk, which is delicately flavoured when fresh, but is stored in brine which makes it salty. It is used in cheese pies, added to salads either crumbled or in slices, and served as an accompaniment to a meal. Feta is now being made by other countries and cow's milk is being used. It is a good idea to taste feta before you buy in case you do not like the type which your store is selling. Feta keeps well in polythene wrapping or a screw-topped jar in the refrigerator. It can be allowed to dry and harden for grating purposes.

Kaséri: A firm, cream-coloured cheese with a mild salty flavour made from sheep's milk. Delicious with bread, olives and a glass of wine. The Italian cheese *provolone* is a good substitute.

Kefalotíri: A hard salty cheese made from sheep's or goat's milk which is often sold as a round head-shaped lump (*kefáli*) from which it derives its name. It is generally grated and used with pasta. Parmesan cheese is a good substitute.

Manúri: An unsalted soft white cheese made from sheep's or goat's milk. It is sometimes mixed with herbs. Unsalted curd cheese is a good substitute.

Mizíthra: An unsalted soft white cheese made from sheep's or goat's milk, though connoisseurs prefer mizithra to be made of sheep's milk. It is eaten on its own or with fruit, honey, and as a savoury cheese with herbs. Substitute fresh cottage cheese, curd cheese or Italian *ricotta*. Like feta, mizithra can be allowed to dry and harden for use as a grating cheese.

Cheese Pie (*Tirópitta*)

1 lb (450 g) feta cheese
3 or 4 eggs
1½ pints (900 ml) white sauce (see p. 131)
½ teaspoon salt

pinch of freshly ground pepper
½ teaspoon grated nutmeg
olive oil
1 lb (450 g) fillo pastry

Mash the cheese with a fork and mix in the eggs and white sauce. Season with salt, pepper and nutmeg. Grease a baking tin and lay in half of the pastry sheets, brushing each sheet with oil. Add the filling and cover with the rest of the pastry sheets. Smear each sheet with oil as you lay it on. Score the top with square patterns to make serving easier. Bake in the oven at 375°F/190°C/Gas 5 until crisp and golden on top (about 30 minutes).

Cretan Cheese Pies (*Kalitsúnia*)

Crete was once considered the centre of the Western world. In his encyclopedic *Natural History*, Pliny (AD 23–79) showed particular interest in the island and according to him Crete was the original home of the cypress tree. No doubt he enjoyed these cheese pies while he went about his work.

2 cups flour
1 teaspoon salt
2 tablespoons clarified butter *or* margarine

1 lb (450 g) mizithra *or* cottage cheese
1 egg, beaten
sesame seeds

Make a dough by sifting the flour with the salt. Rub in the butter and add enough water to make a stiff dough. Cover with a cloth. Mash the cheese and add some dried herb like sage if you like this taste. Roll out the dough to make a thin sheet and cut out rounds about 4–6 inches (10–15 cm) across. Put a portion of cheese on the pastry round and moisten the edges. Fold up and press the edges together with a fork. Put the pies on a greased baking sheet and brush with egg. Sprinkle with sesame seeds. Bake in the oven at 375°F/190°C/Gas 5 until golden (about 30 minutes).

Cheese Triangles (*Tirotrígona*)

1 cup crumbled feta cheese
½ cup mizithra *or* ricotta cheese
2 eggs, beaten
1 tablespoon chopped parsley *or*
  coriander leaf

½ teaspoon freshly ground pepper
½ lb (225 g) fillo pastry
olive oil

Turn on the oven to 350°F/180°C/Gas 4. Beat the cheeses together in a bowl with a fork. Add the eggs, herb and seasoning. Cut the pastry sheets to make strips about 4 inches (10 cm) wide. Put a tablespoon of filling on one end of a strip and fold the end over to form a triangular shape. Continue folding up the triangle. Put the triangles on a greased baking sheet and brush them with oil. Bake in the oven until they are crisp and golden. Serve hot or cold.

If you want to prepare the triangles in advance, keep them in a damp cloth in a cool place or wrapped in plastic in the refrigerator. Brush with oil before baking. This is the basic recipe for the filling, but, as with all fillings, use your imagination and experiment with your own combinations. If you cannot get the Greek cheeses try any locally available goat's milk cheese. Finely chopped nuts or chives could be added to the filling to add texture and taste.

Cheese Rolls (*Burekákia apo Tirí*)

6 oz (170 g) feta cheese
4 oz (110 g) mizithra *or* cottage
  cheese
2 tablespoons clarified butter *or*
  olive oil
2 tablespoons flour
½ cup yogurt

1 egg, beaten
1 tablespoon chopped parsley *or*
  coriander leaf
½ teaspoon grated nutmeg
½ lb (225 g) fillo pastry
clarified butter *or* olive oil for
  brushing

Mash the cheeses together with a fork. Melt the butter and blend in the flour. Add the yogurt, cheese, egg, parsley and nutmeg. Cut the pastry sheets to make pieces about 8 × 12 inches (20 × 30 cm). Lay out a piece on the pastry board and brush with melted butter. Fold in half and brush again. Put a tablespoon of filling on one end of the folded sheet and turn over the end. Fold in the sides and roll up. Put the rolls on a greased baking sheet with the seams underneath. Bake in the oven at 375°F/190°C/Gas 5 until they are crisp and golden (15–25 minutes). Makes about 26.

Baked Cheese (*Féta Fúrno*)

According to Greek mythology, Demeter, the goddess of earth and agriculture, was the protectress of Corfu. Each evening before retiring to Mount Olympus, she would hide her scythe under Corfu. Gradually the island moulded itself to the shape of a scythe so that one of Corfu's early names was Drepani: a scythe. This recipe is a modern version of the traditional way of cooking feta on Corfu.

Wrap a piece of cheese, together with a slice of onion, tomato, marjoram, salt and pepper in tinfoil, and bake in a hot oven for 4–5 minutes. Serve in its packet with a salad or pieces of lightly toasted bread and chopped tomatoes.

Cheese Bread (*Psomí ke Tirí*)

1 long crusty loaf
½ cup sesame paste
2 cloves garlic, finely chopped

½ cup feta, curd *or* cottage cheese
lemon juice

Cut the loaf into thick slices. Mix the sesame paste with garlic and cheese and spread on the slices. Sprinkle with lemon juice. Put under the grill or bake in the oven at 350°F/180°C/Gas 4 for 15 minutes. Cheese bread is delicious served with a bean dish or a thick soup.

By using different cheeses, herbs and other ingredients such as onion or tomato, you can make a range of cheese spreads to use in this way.

Sauces (*Sáltes*)

Egg and Garlic Sauce
(*Sáltsa Avgoskórdho*)

2 eggs, hard-boiled
2–4 cloves garlic
½ teaspoon salt

pinch of marjoram *or* oregano
2 tablespoons lemon juice
4 tablespoons olive oil

Mash the eggs in a bowl with a fork. Pound the garlic in a mortar with the salt and dried herb. Stir into the eggs. Stir in the lemon juice and add the oil gradually, mixing well until a thick sauce is made. Serve with a salad or bean dish.

Egg and Lemon Sauce (*Avgolémono Sáltsa*)

The classic taste of Greek cookery.

1 tablespoon clarified butter *or*
    margarine
2 tablespoons flour
2 cups hot stock

2 eggs
juice of 1 lemon
2 tablespoons cold water

Heat the butter in a small pan and stir in the flour. Gradually add the stock, stirring all the time. Remove from the heat. Beat the eggs well in a bowl and stir in the lemon juice and 2 tablespoons of cold water. Now gradually add the hot stock mixture and return the whole to the pan. Do not allow the sauce to boil or it will curdle.

Thick Egg and Lemon Sauce (*Avgolémono Sáltsa*)

This is a thick egg and lemon sauce for pouring over stuffed vegetables.

3 eggs
1 tablespoon cornflour dissolved in
  2 tablespoons water

juice of 1 lemon
1 cup hot stock

Beat the eggs in a pan until they fluff up. Place on a low heat. Stir in the cornflour liquid. Gradually add the lemon juice. Stir in the stock. Keep stirring over a low heat until the sauce thickens. Do not allow to boil. Pour the sauce over stuffed vegetables or use as a thick gravy or sauce with a bean dish.

Garlic Sauce (*Skordhaliá*)

6 thick slices of bread
3–6 cloves garlic
½ teaspoon salt

2 tablespoons wine vinegar
4 tablespoons olive oil

Break the bread up in a bowl, moisten with warm water and leave to soak. Pound the garlic with the salt. Stir in the vinegar. Squeeze the soaked bread and mash with a fork. Add the pounded garlic and mix well. Gradually add the olive oil until a smooth sauce is made. This can be thinned with hot water if necessary. Use as a dip or pour over fried vegetables.

   The sauce is also traditionally made with potatoes. Boil and mash two potatoes and mix with the garlic and other ingredients. The garlic can be increased according to taste. Again, thin the sauce with water if required.

Greek Mayonnaise (*Mayonéza*)

1 egg
pinch of mustard powder
pinch of salt

2 tablespoons lemon juice
1 tablespoon dried herbs
1 cup olive oil

Beat the ingredients together or blend to make this tasty mayonnaise. Serve with salads and potato dishes.

Oil and Lemon Sauce (*Lemonóladho*)

3 tablespoons olive oil
1 tablespoon lemon juice

pinch of salt
pinch of freshly ground pepper

Beat the ingredients together. Serve with either cooked or raw salads, especially raw cabbage.

Oil and Vinegar Sauce (*Ladhóksidhi*)

2 tablespoons red wine vinegar
½ cup olive oil
1 clove garlic, finely chopped

pinch of freshly ground pepper
½ teaspoon salt

Beat the ingredients together. Serve with uncooked salads.

Sesame Sauce (*Tahíni Sáltsa*)

½ cup sesame paste
juice of 1 lemon
1 clove garlic, finely chopped

2 teaspoons chopped parsley *or*
   coriander leaf

Mix the sesame paste with a cup of warm water. Stir in the lemon juice, garlic and chopped herb.

Tomato Sauce (*Domatósaltsa*)

1 lb (450 g) tomatoes
2 tablespoons olive oil
2 tablespoons finely chopped onion
a few bay leaves
½ teaspoon basil

½ teaspoon salt
pinch of freshly ground pepper
2 teaspoons sugar
small piece cinnamon

Mash the tomatoes with a fork. Heat the oil in a pan and fry the onion for 2 minutes. Add the tomatoes and the rest of the ingredients. Cook together on a gentle heat until the sauce thickens. To give extra flavour, a cup of red wine could be added with the tomatoes.

Serve with cooked vegetables, pasta and cereals.

Tomato and Lentil Sauce (*Domatósaltsa ke Fakkí*)

½ cup olive oil
1 onion, finely chopped
2 cloves garlic, finely chopped
1 cup cooked lentils
½ teaspoon salt

pinch of freshly ground pepper
½ cup red wine
4 tomatoes, chopped
1 teaspoon basil

Heat the oil in a pan with the onion and fry for 2 minutes. Add the garlic, lentils, salt and pepper. Fry for 2 minutes. Add the wine, tomatoes and basil and cook until the sauce thickens. Add a little water if necessary. Serve with pasta or rice dishes.

White Sauce (*Áspri Sáltsa*)

2 tablespoons clarified butter,
  margarine *or* oil
2 tablespoons flour
½ teaspoon salt

pinch of freshly ground pepper
½ teaspoon grated nutmeg
1 pint (600 ml) milk
2 allspice berries (optional)

Heat the butter over a gentle heat in a pan. Stir in the flour, salt, pepper and nutmeg. Stir until well blended. Remove from the heat. Stir in the milk and return to the heat. Cook on a low heat until the sauce is thick and smooth. Add allspice to taste.

Yogurt Sauce (*Yaúrti Sáltsa*)

2 cups yogurt
1 tablespoon honey
2 tablespoons lemon juice
1 spring onion, finely chopped

1 clove garlic, finely chopped
½ teaspoon salt
pinch of freshly ground pepper
1 teaspoon chopped mint leaf

Combine all the ingredients and garnish with the mint leaf.

Yogurt and Almond Sauce
(*Yaúrti ke Amígdhalo Sáltsa*)

2 cups yogurt
½ teaspoon salt
pinch of freshly ground pepper
pinch of dried sage
½ cup blanched almonds

1–2 cloves garlic
2 tablespoons olive oil
1 tablespoon lemon juice
2 teaspoons chopped parsley *or*
  coriander leaf

Beat the yogurt with the salt, pepper and sage. Skin the almonds and pound with the garlic. Stir into the yogurt. Stir in the oil and lemon juice and mix well. Garnish with the chopped herb.

Desserts (*Gliká*)

Custard Pie (*Galatobúreko*)

6 eggs
1 cup sugar
1½ cups rice flour
6 cups milk
1 tablespoon grated lemon peel *or* orange peel
clarified butter *or* margarine

1 lb (450 g) fillo pastry
1 tablespoon rosewater, orange blossom water *or* water
2 cups sugar
1 cup water
1 tablespoon lemon juice

Beat the eggs with the sugar until fluffy. Add the flour, milk and peel. Cook over a low heat until the mixture thickens, stirring to prevent sticking. Remove from the heat and stir in 3 tablespoons melted butter.

Grease a shallow baking tin which is about 8 × 12 inches (20 × 30 cm) and turn the oven on to 375°F/190°C/Gas 5. Put 8–10 sheets of pastry in the bottom of the pan, brushing each sheet with melted butter. They can be allowed to turn up the sides of the dish. Trim at the top of the dish. Add the custard mixture and cover with 8–10 pastry sheets. Again, brush each sheet with melted butter. Cut through a few sheets to make squares for serving. Sprinkle with a little rosewater and bake in the oven until crisp and golden (about 45 minutes). Allow to cool.

Meanwhile make the syrup. Boil the sugar, water and lemon juice together for 5 minutes. Let the syrup cool to lukewarm then pour it over the cooked pie. Galatobureko is usually served cold.

Custard Rolls (*Burekákia apó Kréma*)

6 eggs
1 cup sugar
1½ cups rice flour
6 cups milk
1 tablespoon grated lemon peel *or* orange peel

clarified butter *or* margarine
1 lb (450 g) fillo pastry
2 cups sugar
1 cup water
1 tablespoon lemon juice

This recipe is virtually the same as the previous dish except that the custard filling is put into individual rolls. Beat the eggs with the sugar until fluffy. Add the flour, milk and peel. Cook over a low heat for 15 minutes, stirring all the time to prevent sticking. Remove from the heat and stir in a tablespoon of butter. Allow to cool or put in the refrigerator to thicken.

Cut the pastry sheets to make pieces about 8 × 12 inches (20 × 30 cm). Lay out a piece on the pastry board and brush with melted butter. Fold in half and brush again. Put a tablespoon of cooled custard filling on one end of the folded sheet and turn over the end. Fold in the sides and roll up. Put the rolls on greased baking sheets with the seams underneath. Bake in the oven at 375°F/190°C/Gas 5 until they are crisp and golden (about 15 minutes).

Meanwhile make the syrup. Boil the sugar, water and lemon juice together for 5 minutes. Let the syrup cool to lukewarm then pour it over the cooked rolls.

Cheese and Honey Pie (*Tirí ke Melópitta*)

1 lb (450 g) mizithra *or* ricotta cheese
½ cup honey
3 eggs, beaten
1 teaspoon grated lemon peel

clarified butter *or* margarine
1 lb (450 g) fillo pastry
1 tablespoon rosewater, orange blossom water *or* water

Mix the cheese, honey, eggs and lemon peel in a bowl. Grease a 9-inch (23-cm) pie dish or small baking dish and put in 8–10 sheets of fillo. Brush each sheet with melted butter. Trim the sheets as they reach the edge of the dish. Add the cheese mixture and cover with 8–10 pastry sheets, brushing each sheet with melted butter. Press the edges of the pastry together and sprinkle with rosewater. Bake in the oven at 375°F/190°C/Gas 5 until the top is crisp and golden (about 45 minutes).

Rice Pudding (*Rizógalo*)

½ cup rice
2 pints (1200 ml) milk
½ cup sugar

1 teaspoon grated lemon peel
ground cinnamon

Wash the rice and leave to soak for 30 minutes. Drain and put ½ cup water to boil. Put in the rice, milk, sugar and lemon. Cook over a gentle heat until the mixture is thick and creamy. Serve sprinkled with cinnamon.

Other flavours could be added to this dish. Pieces of cinnamon could be cooked with the rice. Grated nutmeg could be sprinkled on. Serve with fruit and nuts.

Chestnut Pudding (*Kréma Kástana*)

2 lb (900 g) cooked chestnuts
½ cup Greek brandy
½ cup sugar
2 cups double cream

1 tablespoon ouzo
1 tablespoon chopped pistachio
   nuts *or* walnuts

Mash the chestnuts in a bowl and stir in the brandy and sugar. Beat the cream until fluffy, gradually adding the ouzo. Beat together with the chestnut mixture and sprinkle with the chopped nuts. Serve chilled.

Dried Fruit Salad (*Frúta Ksirá Saláta*)

½ cup dried figs
½ cup dried apricots
½ cup sultanas
1 tablespoon sliced blanched
   almonds

pinch of ground aniseed *or* fennel
   seed
1–2 tablespoons ouzo

Wash the dried fruits and leave to soak overnight in water or a mixture of diluted grape juice. Next day simmer gently in a pan for 10 minutes. Put in a serving dish with the juice. Sprinkle with the nuts and ground aniseed. Add ouzo to taste.

Ouzo is particularly good with figs, but you may prefer brandy or sherry to the strong taste of aniseed.

Fruit Fritters (*Tiganítes*)

1½ cups flour
2 teaspoons baking powder
2 tablespoons sugar
1 egg, beaten
½ cup milk
3 tablespoons chopped apple

3 tablespoons chopped dried
 apricot
olive oil for deep-frying
honey
ground cinnamon
lemon juice

Sift the flour with the baking powder and sugar. Beat the egg into the milk and add to the flour. Add enough water to make a thick creamy batter. Put in the fruit. Heat the oil in a deep-frying pan. Drop in spoonfuls of the fruit batter and fry until they are golden. Remove and drain on absorbent paper. Serve with honey, cinnamon and lemon juice.

The same batter may be used to make fritters from pieces of fruit. Dip the pieces in batter and deep-fry.

Cretan Pancakes (*Tiganítes*)

4 oz (110 g) flour
pinch of salt
1 egg
½ pint (300 ml) liquid (⅔ milk, ⅓
 water)
8 oz (225 g) mizithra *or* cottage
 cheese

honey
lemon juice
clarified butter, margarine *or* olive
 oil

Make the batter by sifting the flour and salt together in a bowl. Drop in the egg and beat the mixture well. Gradually beat in just enough liquid to make a stiff batter. Beat until smooth and leave to stand for 5 minutes. Gradually beat in the rest of the liquid.

Have the cheese, honey and lemon juice ready to serve immediately the pancakes are cooked. Heat ½ tablespoon butter in a frying pan and add enough batter to cover the bottom of the pan. Cook on each side until golden (about 1½–2 minutes). Remove and put a little cheese and honey on each pancake. Roll up and put on a warm dish. Serve with lemon juice or lemon wedges.

Creamed Apricots (*Veríkokko Kréma*)

1 lb (450 g) dried apricots
½ cup sugar

½ cup ground almonds
1 cup double cream

Cover the apricots with water and leave to soak overnight. Next day simmer gently until they are soft. Add the sugar and almonds and mix together until all the ingredients are well blended. Stir in the cream and allow to cool. Serve chilled.

Peach Compote (*Rodhákina Kombósta*)

2 lb (900 g) fresh peaches, cut in
   half and stoned
juice of 1 lemon

½ cup sugar
finely crushed ice

Put the peaches in a pan and squash with a wooden spoon. Add a cup of water and the lemon juice. Sprinkle the sugar on and cook on a gentle heat until the peaches are tender. Allow to cool and serve chilled with crushed ice.

Melon with Honey Dressing (*Pepóni me Melósaltsa*)

1 melon
2 tablespoons clear honey
2 tablespoons lemon juice

4 tablespoons Greek brandy *or*
   sherry

Cut the melon in half and remove the seeds. Cut the melon in pieces for serving. Arrange on a dish. Make up the syrup by mixing the honey, lemon juice and brandy. Pour it over the melon slices when serving.
   Allow a quarter of a melon per person.

Fresh Fruit (*Frúta Fréska*)

Fresh fruit is as much a part of any meal as a cooked dessert would be. It is particularly welcome after a filling meal or during the summer months. Wash the fruit you can obtain in season and arrange carefully on a bowl without drying the fruit. This greatly enhances the thirst-quenching appearance of a bowl of fruit. Arrange them on a bed of green leaves and have little bowls of warm water for each diner into which you squeeze a little lemon juice, rosewater or orange blossom water for cleaning the fingers.

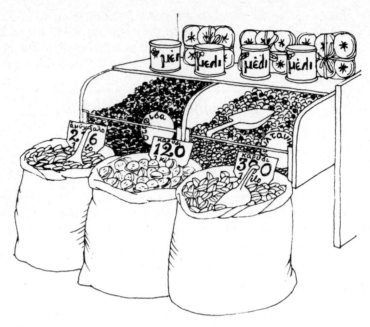

Cakes and Sweets (*Glíkismata ke Zaharotá*)

Greeks love to eat out, especially with plenty of friends or relatives. It is often the custom to leave the restaurant or taverna before the dessert and eat this at a special pastry shop and café, the *zaharoplastío*. Here you can buy all kinds of cakes and sweetmeats as well as coffee and drinks. This custom adds extra interest to your night out, giving you a change of scenery as well as of menu!

Honey Cake (*Melópitta*)

½ lb (225 g) flour
2 teaspoons baking powder
½ teaspoon ground cinnamon
pinch of salt
5 oz (140 g) clarified butter *or* margarine
2½ oz (70 g) sugar
3 tablespoons thick honey

2 eggs
4 tablespoons milk *or* yogurt
2 tablespoons rosewater *or* orange blossom water
2 tablespoons thin honey
1 tablespoon finely chopped walnuts *or* almonds

Turn on the oven to 400°F/200°C/Gas 6. Sift the flour with the baking powder, cinnamon and salt. Cream the butter, sugar and thick honey together in a mixing bowl. Beat in the eggs and fold in the flour. Add the milk. Mix well until the cake mixture is thick and creamy. Put in a greased 7-inch (18-cm) cake tin. Bake in the middle of the oven for 1 hour. Test with a fork to see if the cake is ready. It should come out clean. Allow to cool and remove from the tin. Put on a dish.

Make up a syrup with rosewater and honey. Put in a pan and warm gently. Pour the warm syrup over the cake and sprinkle with the chopped nuts.

Lemon Cake (*Lemonópitta*)

7 tablespoons clarified butter *or* margarine
¾ cup sugar
2 eggs, beaten
½ cup warm milk
1½ cups flour

1½ teaspoons baking powder
pinch of salt
1 tablespoon grated lemon peel
½ cup lemon juice
1 cup icing sugar

Turn on the oven to 350°F/180°C/Gas 4. Cream the butter by beating in a bowl. Gradually beat in the sugar. Fold the eggs into the butter mixture with a spoon. Stir in the milk and then the flour, baking powder, salt and grated lemon peel. Mix well to make a batter. Pour into a greased shallow baking tin of about 8 × 12 inches (20 × 30 cm). Bake in the oven for 25 minutes. Stir the lemon juice with the icing sugar. Take the cake from the oven 5 minutes before it is ready, and spoon the topping over. Put the cake back in the oven to complete the baking. Test for readiness with a fork. The prongs should come out clean. Allow the cake to cool and cut in squares to serve.

Lenten Cake (*Pítta Nistísimi*)

Zákinthos, the most southerly of the Ionian Islands, was known as Zante to the Venetians who ruled there between 1479 and 1797. They enjoyed the mild climate so much that they called the island 'Zante – fior di Levante'. Currants grow well here and are gathered in August when fully ripe and spread out to dry in the sun for three weeks. Currants from Zante have been exported to England since the sixteenth century when they were also made into wine. The word *currant* seems to be a corruption of the French *raisins de Corinthe*.

The main town of the island, Zakinthos, has a museum with a fine collection of icons and frescoes, many of which depict traditional Lenten scenes as well as Saint Dionysus, the patron saint of the island.

3 cups flour
2 teaspoons baking powder
1 teaspoon cinnamon powder
½ teaspoon grated nutmeg
2 tablespoons currants
2 tablespoons sultanas *or* raisins
2 tablespoons chopped walnuts,
  hazelnuts *or* almonds

6 tablespoons olive oil *or*
  margarine
1 cup sugar
2 tablespoons lemon juice
1 tablespoon grated lemon peel

Sift the flour with the baking powder, cinnamon and nutmeg. Add the currants, sultanas and nuts. Beat together the oil, sugar, lemon juice and lemon peel in a bowl. Add the flour and fruits and mix well. Grease a shallow baking dish about 8 × 12 inches (20 × 30 cm) and pour in the cake mixture. Bake in the oven at 375°F/190°C/Gas 5 for about 45 minutes. Test for readiness with a fork which should come out clean. Allow to cool before cutting.

Sesame Cake (*Tahinópitta*)

3 cups flour
2 teaspoons baking powder
1 teaspoon salt
½ teaspoon powdered aniseed
1 cup sugar
2 tablespoons sultanas

2 tablespoons chopped walnuts,
  hazelnuts *or* almonds
1 tablespoon grated lemon peel
2 tablespoons lemon juice
1 cup water
1 cup sesame paste

Sift the flour with the baking powder, salt and aniseed. Add the sugar and sultanas, nuts and lemon peel. Mix well. Stir the lemon juice and water gradually into the sesame paste. Mix in the flour and fruit and blend well. Grease a shallow baking dish about 8 × 12 inches (20 × 30 cm) and pour in the cake mixture. Bake in the oven at 375°F/190°C/ Gas 5 for about 45 minutes. Test for readiness with a fork which should come out clean. Allow to cool before cutting.

New Year's Cake (*Vasilópitta*)

Saint Basil is the patron saint of the New Year and his day is celebrated all over Greece. Early on New Year's Eve relations and friends gather for drinks and sweetmeats. Children may go from house to house singing the songs of St Basil and wishing those at home good fortune in the coming year. At the stroke of midnight the cake is brought in to be cut. Outside the bells are ringing, guns go off, fireworks crack, everyone wishes *'Hroniá pollá!'* (literally 'Many years') and waits to see who has the slice with the gold coin or charm in it. This lucky person will have good fortune for the whole year. St Basil brings sweets and little presents for the children on New Year's Eve. Here is his cake.

8 oz (225 g) clarified butter *or* margarine	10 oz (280 g) flour
	2 teaspoons baking powder
6 oz (170 g) sugar	4 tablespoons milk
grated peel and juice of 1 lemon	1 tablespoon icing sugar
4 eggs	

Beat the butter and sugar until light and creamy. Add the lemon and beat in the eggs. Sift the flour with the baking powder and fold into the mixture. Stir in the milk. Grease a 10-inch (25-cm) cake tin and put in the cake mixture. Put in a gold or silver coin or token. Bake in the middle of the oven at 375°F/190°C/Gas 5 for 1 hour 5 minutes. Serve the cake dusted with icing sugar. A little more richness may be added by putting in a small glass of Greek brandy with the milk.

St Basil's Yeast Cake

Some families bake a yeast cake for New Year's Eve. Here is a typical recipe.

6 oz (170 g) clarified butter *or* margarine	1½ cups warm milk
	1 lb (450 g) flour
6 oz (170 g) sugar	½ teaspoon salt
1 tablespoon honey	1 teaspoon ground cinnamon
2 eggs	1 lb (450 g) dried fruit
1 tablespoon dried yeast	

Beat the butter and sugar together until light and creamy. Add the honey and beat in the eggs. Put the yeast in a small jug and pour on 1 cup of the warm milk. Allow it to double its volume (about 10 minutes) and then add to the butter and sugar mixture. Sift the flour with the salt and cinnamon, add the dried fruit and add to the rest of the mixture. Stir in the rest of the milk. Pour the mixture into a large cake tin which has been greased and floured and bake in the oven at 400°F/200°C/Gas 6 for 1 hour. Put in the gold or silver coin or token before the cake is cooked.

Walnut Cake (*Karidhópitta*)

8 oz (225 g) clarified butter *or*
  margarine
5 oz (140 g) sugar
1 teaspoon grated orange peel
4 eggs
14 oz (400 g) flour
3 teaspoons baking powder
½ teaspoon salt

1 cup chopped walnuts
1½ cups milk

For the syrup:
2 cups sugar
1 cup water
juice of 1 lemon

Cream the butter by beating with the sugar. Add the orange peel and beat in the eggs. Sift the flour with the baking powder and salt and mix in the chopped nuts. Add some of this to the butter mixture and then add some of the milk. Keep doing this until all the flour and milk have been blended into the cream. Put the mixture in a large cake tin or baking dish which has been greased and floured. Bake in the middle of the oven at 375°F/190°C/ Gas 5 for 1 hour. Meanwhile make the syrup. Boil the sugar, water and lemon juice for 5 minutes. Pour the slightly cooled syrup over the cake, allow to cool and cut in squares. Serve with fresh cream.

Yogurt Cake (*Yaurtópitta*)

4 oz (110 g) clarified butter *or*
  margarine
8 oz (225 g) sugar
1 cup yogurt
3 eggs
1 tablespoon grated lemon peel
8 oz (225 g) flour
1 teaspoon baking powder

For the syrup:
2 cups sugar
1 cup water
juice of ½ lemon

Turn on the oven to 350°F/180°C/Gas 4. Cream the butter by beating with the sugar until light and fluffy. Add the yogurt and mix well. Beat in the eggs and lemon peel. Sift the flour with the baking powder and fold into the butter and yogurt mixture. Grease a cake tin or baking dish and pour in the cake mixture. Bake for 1–1¼ hours. Meanwhile make the syrup. Boil the sugar, water and lemon juice for 5 minutes. Pour the lukewarm syrup over the cooked cake.

This cake can be made more substantial by adding ½ cup of ground almonds before you fold in the flour.

Nut Pastry (*Baklavá*)

One of the best-known Greek sweetmeats made with fillo pastry, honey and nuts. Make the day before it is required.

clarified butter *or* margarine
1 cup sugar
1 cup hot water
2 cups chopped blanched almonds
   or walnuts
1 lb (450 g) fillo pastry
powdered cinnamon

For the syrup:
1 cup sugar
1 cup honey
1 cup water
juice of 1 lemon

Heat 4 tablespoons of melted butter in a pan with the sugar and 1 cup of hot water. Add the chopped nuts. Grease a baking tin large enough to take the fillo sheets. Put in 3 sheets, brushing each sheet with melted butter. Spread on a thin layer of the nut mixture, sprinkle with a little cinnamon and cover with 2 more sheets of buttered fillo. Keep adding alternate layers of filling and pastry and cover with 3 sheets. Brush the top with melted butter and score a diamond pattern on the top to aid serving. Bake in the oven at 375°F/190°C/Gas 5 until crisp and golden (about 30 minutes).

   Meanwhile make the syrup. Boil the sugar, honey, water and lemon juice for 5 minutes. Allow to cool a little then pour over the cooked pastry. This tastes best the next day because the syrup has had a chance to soak into the pastry. Baklava is also delicious eaten hot with some aromatic rosewater or orange blossom water sprinkled over it and served with chilled cream. A real treat!

Nut Rolls (*Plakúndes*)

The basic idea of these sweetmeats is to put a spoon of spiced ground nuts on a strip of fillo pastry, turn in the sides and roll up. Bake them and cover with syrup after baking.

8 oz (225 g) ground almonds *or*
   other nuts
½ teaspoon grated nutmeg
1 teaspoon powdered cinnamon
2 teaspoons honey
1 egg, beaten
8 oz (225 g) fillo pastry
clarified butter *or* margarine

For the syrup:
2 cups sugar
1 cup water
juice of ½ lemon
1 tablespoon rosewater *or* orange
   blossom water

Turn on the oven to 350°F/180°C/Gas 4. Mix the nuts, nutmeg, cinnamon and honey. Stir in the egg. Cut the pastry into strips about 6 inches (15 cm) wide. Brush with melted butter and fold over. Brush again and put on a spoonful of nut mixture. Fold over the end, fold in the sides and roll up. Put the rolls on a greased baking sheet with the seams underneath. Bake in the oven until crisp and golden (15–20 minutes).

Meanwhile make the syrup. Boil the ingredients together for 5 minutes. Allow to cool a little and pour it over the cooked rolls.

Sweet Cheese Rolls (*Bugátsa*)

8 oz (225 g) mizithra *or* soft cheese
1 tablespoon finely chopped
  pistachio nuts *or* ground
  almonds

½ teaspoon powdered cinnamon
1 tablespoon honey
8 oz (225 g) fillo pastry
clarified butter *or* margarine

Turn on the oven to 375°F/190°C/Gas 5. Stir the cheese with the nuts, cinnamon and honey. Cut the pastry into strips about 6 inches (15 cm) wide. Brush each strip with melted butter and fold over. Brush again and add a spoonful of cheese mixture. Fold over one end, fold in the sides and roll up. Put the rolls on a greased baking sheet with the seams underneath. Bake in the oven until crisp and golden (15–20 minutes).

Easter Bracelets (*Kulurákia*)

A favourite with children at Eastertime. The pastry can be made into different shapes, but children like the ring-shaped ones that will fit tiny wrists or through which they can stick their fingers.

4 oz (110 g) clarified butter *or*
  margarine
4 oz (110 g) sugar
½ teaspoon vanilla extract
2 eggs
12 oz (340 g) flour
2 teaspoons baking powder

½ teaspoon powdered cinnamon
sesame seeds

For the glaze:
1 egg, beaten
1 tablespoon milk

Beat the butter until it is creamy. Beat in the sugar and vanilla extract. Add the eggs one at a time and beat in well. Sift the flour with the baking powder and cinnamon and stir into the butter and eggs to make a soft dough. Allow the dough to stand for 30 minutes. Break off walnut-sized pieces and make a roll about 4 inches (10 cm) long.

Pinch the ends together to form a bracelet and flatten slightly. Put the sesame seeds on a plate and dip one side of the bracelets in the seeds to coat. Place on a greased baking sheet.

Make the glaze by beating another egg with the milk. Brush each bracelet. Bake in the oven at 375°F/190°C/Gas 5 until golden (15–20 minutes). Allow to cool on a wire rack and store in an airtight tin.

Shortbread (*Kurabiédhes*)

These Greek shortbreads are a favourite on New Year's Day and at Christmas. At Christmastime each shortbread will have a clove stuck into it to signify the spices brought by the three kings to Bethlehem. In village bakeries you will find them in tins or baskets of fine sugar.

4 oz (110 g) clarified butter *or* margarine
2 oz (50 g) caster sugar
1 teaspoon ouzo *or* Greek brandy
4 oz (110 g) flour

2 oz (50 g) rice flour
pinch of salt
rosewater *or* orange blossom water
icing sugar

Beat the butter with the sugar until light and creamy. Add the ouzo. Sift the flour, rice flour and salt and fold into the butter. Knead into a smooth lump. The biscuit dough can now be rolled out and cut into diamond shapes or pieces broken off to make crescents or moons. Put the biscuits on to greased baking sheets and bake in the oven at 400°F/200°C/Gas 6 for 15 minutes. Dip the cooked biscuits lightly in rosewater and roll in sugar. Brown sugar can easily be made into powder form for this purpose. Store in an airtight tin with plenty of powdered sugar.

Lover's Knots (*Dhíples*)

2 egg yolks
2 tablespoons sugar
2 tablespoons clarified butter *or* margarine
grated peel of 1 small orange
2 tablespoons ouzo *or* Greek brandy
flour

pinch of salt
olive oil *or* other vegetable oil for deep-frying
1 cup honey
1 cup finely chopped walnuts *or* almonds
powdered cinnamon

Beat the egg yolks gently with the sugar, butter, orange peel and ouzo. Sift 2 cups of flour with the salt and work into the mixture until a stiff dough is formed. Roll out on a floured board and cut into strips about 1 inch (2.5 cm) wide. Tie the strips into knots or bows. Heat the oil in a deep-frying pan and deep-fry the knots until golden. They fry quickly and should be removed before they become too brown. Drain on absorbent paper and arrange on a serving dish. Sprinkle with thin honey, nuts and cinnamon. Do this with each layer of lover's knots.

Honey Doughnuts (*Lukumádhes*)

One of the most delicious Greek sweetmeats, well worth leaving a space for at the end of your meal. You can buy a plate of these at the *zaharoplastío*. They come hot to the table and are delicious with Greek brandy, raki or fruit juice. At other times of the day you can have them with coffee at a coffee shop.

1 tablespoon dried yeast	olive oil *or* other vegetable oil for
1 teaspoon sugar	deep-frying
1 cup warm water	honey
8 oz (225 g) flour	powdered cinnamon
½ teaspoon salt	

Put the yeast in a mixing bowl with the sugar and pour on the warm water. Add 2 oz (50 g) of the flour and beat the batter until smooth. Cover with a cloth and leave in a warm place for the batter to double its size. Add the salt and the rest of the flour and enough water to make a thick batter. Cover and allow to rise again and begin to bubble. This can take from 1–2 hours.

Heat the oil in a deep-frying pan and when the oil is hot drop in spoons of the thick batter using two teaspoons. The dough will puff up and turn light brown. Remove with a perforated spoon or strainer and put on a serving dish. Spoon honey over the lukumadhes and sprinkle on a little cinnamon powder. Serve hot.

A good test for the batter: when it is pinched between finger and thumb it should stretch a little before it breaks.

Sesame Slices (*Paksimádhia*)

6 oz (170 g) flour	2 tablespoons sugar
2½ tablespoons sesame seeds	4 tablespoons clarified butter *or*
4 tablespoons clear honey	margarine

Turn on the oven to 350°F/180°C/Gas 4. Use a little butter to grease a baking sheet or shallow baking tin. Mix all the ingredients and spread onto the sheet. Bake in the oven until golden (20–25 minutes). Leave to cool for 5 minutes. Cut in squares. Put on a wire rack and allow to cool. Makes 24.

Semolina Halva (*Halvás*)

4 tablespoons clarified butter *or* margarine
1 cup semolina
1 cup sugar
4 cloves
small piece of cinnamon

1 tablespoon almonds, blanched and sliced
1 tablespoon rosewater *or* orange blossom water
1 tablespoon pistachio nuts *or* pine nuts, finely chopped

Heat the butter in a pan and fry the semolina gently until it begins to turn golden. Add the sugar, cloves, cinnamon and 2 cups of water. Cook on a low heat until the mixture thickens. Add the almonds and rosewater and continue cooking until a lump is formed. Turn out on to a greased dish and flatten. Sprinkle with the chopped pistachio nuts. Serve hot or cold with cream.

Spoon Sweets, Preserves (*Glikó Kutaliú*)

The Greeks have a special way with jam. Traditionally, guests are first offered a spoonful of jam and a glass of water. This may be followed by a small drink or cup of Greek coffee. In a hot climate, particularly if you have walked some distance to your host's house, the spoon sweet followed by a glass of cooled water has a restorative and cheering effect which is positively magical!

The rules for making Greek preserves are similar to ordinary jam-making procedure. Switch the oven on to a low heat. Put your jars with their lids on a rack in the oven. Screw-top jars are excellent for jam-making, especially the type which have thin rubber or plastic washers welded to the lid. A simple test to see if jam is ready is to put a drop on a cold plate. Push it with the forefinger. If the jam crinkles it is ready. Pour into hot jars and seal immediately. Sealing hot jam as soon as possible avoids any possibility of it going mouldy since a vacuum is created as the jam cools. There is no need to use white sugar in jam-making since there are now many varieties of unrefined sugars at reasonable prices on the market.

Apricot Preserve (*Veríkokko Glikó*)

2 lb (900 g) fresh apricots
½ pint (300 ml) water

grated rind and juice of 1 lemon
2 lb (900 g) sugar

Wash the apricots and cut in half. Remove the stones. Put in a preserving pan with the water and lemon. Heat gently until the apricots begin to soften. Add the sugar and continue cooking on a gentle heat. After 30 minutes test the jam for setting point. Pour into hot jars, seal and allow to cool. Label and store in a cool place.

Quince Preserve (*Kidhóni Glikó*)

3 lb (1.35 kg) quinces
4 cups sugar

a few fresh geranium leaves *or*
pieces of cinnamon
juice of 1 lemon

Peel the quinces and cut in half. Core, then cut in pieces. Put in a preserving pan with a cup of water, cover and cook on a low heat until the fruit is tender. Remove from the heat and add the sugar and geranium leaves or cinnamon sticks. Raise the heat a little and cook until the jam thickens, stirring from time to time. Add the lemon juice. Test a little of the jam by putting a drop on a cold plate. Push the drop with the finger. When it crinkles, the jam is ready. Pour into hot jars, seal and allow to cool. Label and store in a cool place.

Aubergine Preserve (*Melitzanáki Glikó*)

This preserve, which is particularly liked in Crete, is made with tiny aubergines. If you cannot obtain them, here is a recipe which uses aubergine cut in pieces. Otherwise use the same weight of tiny aubergines.

2 lb (900 g) aubergines
2 lemons
blanched almonds
2 lb (900 g) sugar

½ pint (300 ml) water
½ cup honey
small piece of cinnamon
4 cloves

Wash the aubergines and trim. Cut in walnut-sized pieces. Cover with water and the juice of 1 lemon and leave to soak for an hour. Boil until the pieces are just tender (about 10 minutes), remove and drain. Push an almond inside each of the aubergine pieces.

In a preserving pan heat the sugar and water and add the aubergine. Heat gently for 10 minutes. Leave in the syrup overnight. Next day heat the syrup and add the rest of the ingredients, including the juice of the second lemon. Simmer gently until setting point is reached. Test in the usual way and put in hot jars. Seal and allow to cool. Label and store in a cool place.

Greek Coffee

Yannis was a quiet man. Every morning he was up early and by
the time I got up to shower he had breakfasted and was sitting
gazing out over the town which straggled down to the sea. He
would sit like that for hours, his grey head never moving. In the
evening he watered the huge pots of geraniums which stood along
the verandah and brought us bottles of chilled water when we
returned to our room.

One afternoon he rose from his siesta to find me sitting writing
in the shade. 'Would you like some coffee? Greek coffee?' he
asked. 'It will . . . er . . .' He waved his hand and went to fetch
his 'lexicon'. 'It will *revive* you,' he smiled.

'Will you show me how to make it?'

He chuckled and took me to the little outdoor kitchen. The
walls were whitewashed and a vine was beginning to creep over.
He lit a butane gas hob and took out the copper *bríki* from a
cupboard in the dim inner kitchen.

'Fill the pot with as many cups of water as you want. Put in
some sugar if you like it.' Delicately, his large hands set the pot
on the fire. His movements were slow and relaxed. In moments
the water boiled. He removed the pot. 'Now put in a teaspoon of
coffee for each cup and stir it in.' He set the pot on the fire again
and allowed it to boil. He removed the pot immediately and then
allowed the coffee to boil for a second time. Now it had a nice
layer of froth on the top. Yannis pointed to it and smiled. '*To
kaimáki.*' He put out two cups and poured the coffee so that we
each had a share of the froth.

We sat in the shade of the verandah and noisily sipped our coffee
in the Greek manner. Shyly, Yannis began to talk about himself.
He was very fond of Macedonia and had spent fifteen years in
Thessaloniki (Salonica), Greece's second city. He took up my map
of Greece and pointed. After Thessaloniki he was given a senior
post at Kastoria, not far from the Albanian border. Now he had
retired to live with his parents in southern Crete. What was his
job, I asked. He seemed like a farmer or perhaps a carpenter.

He looked at me carefully, watching for my reaction. Then,
screwing up his eyes, as if in pain, he said: 'I was a policeman.'

Drinks (*Potá*)

Water (*Neró*)

Water is excellent.
Pindar, *Olympian Odes 1.i.*

Most of the water in Greece is indeed excellent since it comes from underground springs. Cretans, who particularly prize their water, consider it the national drink. A glass of water should accompany a cup of Greek coffee, a spoon sweet, a meal and any alcoholic drink.

Lemonade (*Lemonádha*)

Mix chilled water with fresh lemon juice in proportions to taste. Add sugar, but not too much. Serve in glasses with mint leaves on the top.

Yogurt (*Yaúrti*)

For each glass of yogurt drink beat ½ glass yogurt with ½ glass cold water. Stir in dried herbs if you like the taste, and a few drops of lemon juice.

Herb Tea (*Hórto Tsái*)

Before tea became widely known in Greece, it was the custom to drink herbal teas or tisanes made from wild aromatic herbs. Originally prescribed by ancient Greek doctors as herbal remedies, they soon became popular as reviving, refreshing as well as healing drinks. If you can collect your own dried herbs, let a sprig infuse in a cup of boiling water for a few minutes. A simple recipe is 1–2 teaspoons of dried herb per cup or 1 tablespoon fresh herb per cup. Put the herbs in a warm earthenware teapot and pour on boiling water. Stir and let the tea infuse for 5 minutes. Strain and serve in tea cups or thick glasses without milk or sugar. Sip while the tea is hot.

Aniseed Tea

For each cup use 1 teaspoon tea and ½ teaspoon ground aniseed. An excellent digestive.

Borage Tea

Infuse 1 teaspoon dried borage leaves or 1 tablespoon fresh borage leaves for 5 minutes. Strain before serving. Borage leaf tea has a mild diuretic effect. It cools the blood system and is used for urinary inflammations.

Dandelion Tea

Cover 1 tablespoon torn fresh dandelion leaves with 2 cups of boiling water. Infuse for 10 minutes. Strain before serving. Dandelion is a strong diuretic and a blood cleanser.

Geranium Tea

Geraniums are grown everywhere in Greece. It is hardly surprising that the leaves and the flowers have been used to make tea. For each cup use 1 teaspoon of tea and 1 geranium leaf. Strain before serving.

Marjoram Tea

Aphrodite took *rígani* from the depths of the ocean to the top of the highest mountain where it would be closest to the rays of the sun. A good tip for herb growers – most of them like the sun!

Infuse 1 teaspoon of dried leaves in 1 cup of boiling water for 5 minutes. Strain. This tea is said to be good for nervous headaches, indigestion, morning sickness in pregnancy, and for calming anxiety.

Mint Tea

Infuse a tablespoon of fresh mint leaf or a teaspoon of dried leaf for 5 minutes. Strain before serving. Mint tea is an excellent digestive and restorative in hot weather.

Parsley Tea

Mentioned many times by Homer, this prolific herb has leaves rich in vitamins and iron. The tea is good for the kidneys, gall bladder, rheumatic conditions and anaemia. Pour a cup of boiling water over a teaspoon of dried leaves and infuse for 2 minutes. Strain before serving.

Rosemary Tea

Make in the same way as parsley tea for headaches, stomach upsets and colds.

Sage Tea

Scorned by Zorba, sage tea (*faskomílo*) is nevertheless still very popular in Cretan villages and other mountainous regions. Sage tea is an excellent tonic and restorative and is given in times of stress or shock. Infuse a teaspoon of dried herb or a tablespoon of fresh.

Thyme Tea

An infusion of thyme is good for coughs and colds. It also relieves sore throats and catarrh. Infuse 2 teaspoons of dried herb for 5 minutes. Strain before serving.

Greek Coffee (*Kafé Ellinikó*)

Not just a drink, more a way of life!
   Ideally, the coffee beans should be roasted, allowed to cool, then ground to a powder just before brewing with or without sugar. Most

people will use ready-ground coffee which is available in vacuum-sealed packs. These should be purchased in small amounts since the aroma (perhaps the most important ingredient of the coffee) soon escapes. Once opened, keep your coffee refrigerated.

Greek coffee is brewed in a coffee pot, originally made of brass or tinned copper but now widely available in aluminium or stainless steel, called a *bríki*. They can now be bought in Greek or Middle Eastern stores if you have not been lucky enough to buy one in Greece. This little pot has a wide flat bottom which tapers to a neck and then widens again towards the rim. A long handle is fixed to the rim so that the pot can be held without burning the fingers. Brikia are made in different sizes according to the number of cups to be served. The cup size is very small, like the Italian *espresso* cup. The shape of the rim allows the coffee to foam during the brewing to make a creamy froth (*kaimáki*). This should be shared between all the cups. Coffee is made according to personal preference. You should ask for *skéto* (without sugar), *métrio* (medium sweet) or *glikó* (sweet). If you do not state a preference you will probably be served with sweet coffee.

Use 1 teaspoon of Greek coffee (more or less according to taste) per cup and 1 cup of water. Put the water in the briki with any sugar and bring to the boil. Remove from the heat and add the coffee. Stir in and allow to boil. As soon as it foams up remove from the heat. Do this again and serve with a glass of water.

Coffee-drinking in Greece, like the tea ceremony of Japan, is part of an unhurried way of life and it can take place at any time of day or night. The cup is small, the taste is delicate. Take your time and savour each sip. Greeks take the opportunity to chat with friends, watch the world go by or simply gaze into space. The coffee should be sipped noisily. This sieving action allows the coffee to be drunk piping hot and it also ensures that you do not drink the coffee grounds which settle in the bottom third of the cup. Apart from its social function, the Greek way of drinking is essentially relaxing, therapeutic, and easily becomes a form of meditation. You have probably never noticed the beauty of a dusty street or the mystery of a pot of geraniums until you have spent those dreamy hours gazing with your little cup of coffee.

Ouzo (*Úzo*)

The usual Greek apéritif is ouzo, a clear, aniseed-flavoured spirit containing 50° alcohol which is distilled from grapes. It is usually taken without water, unlike the *anis* of France, though the practice of making the drink cloudy with water is growing. It is an excellent apéritif in that it does not spoil the palate. Ouzo should be drunk with a few titbits (*mezédhes*) which are mentioned in the chapter on *Appetizers*.

In country areas a drink somewhat similar to ouzo is distilled known as *ráki*. This may or may not be flavoured with aniseed. Raki is even more powerful than ouzo and should be taken in congenial company.

Wine (*Krasí*)

Hippocrates, who came from the island of Kos, affirmed the wholesomeness of wine in times of sickness and in health. The only proviso was that it should be consumed at the right time and in the right quantity to suit individual needs.

Wine was drunk in classical times at festivals and during religious rituals. Dionysus was the god who protected vineyards and presided over the making of wine and over its consumption. Greek wine-making methods were taken up by the Romans and traditional recipes were maintained until the collapse of the Byzantine Empire. During the 400-year rule of the Muslim Turks, Greeks had a harder time in preserving the wine industry.

Most households which have their own vineyard make their own wine which is ready for drinking by the end of the autumn. Some years it will be sweet and at other times dry. Most good Greek wine is, however, always full-bodied, rich and smooth. The grape harvest comes in late summer to autumn. Families harvest their own grapes which are carried in baskets by the donkey or truck to the village to be crushed in the *linós* – a square stone trough with a spout. The crushed juice runs into a copper container, the *kasáni*. From here it is poured into wooden barrels to ferment. The barrels have been washed out with water which has often had sage, pine needles, borage or some other herb added to it as a disinfectant. This gives a special perfume to the wine as it ferments.

The Greek liking for resinated wines dates back to ancient times, shown by the remains of resin found in excavated wine jars. Nine different species of pine grow in Greece. The resin from any of these pines may be used, but the most common resin used is taken from the Jerusalem pine (*Pinus halepensis*). The addition of resin to wine during fermentation, which gives it its characteristic taste, helps to preserve it in hot weather. Resinated wine (*retsína*) is best drunk chilled and is at its most palatable in a hot climate rather than a cold one.

A wide variety of wines is produced in Greece and only a few of them are known abroad. Try as many as you can from the mainland and the islands to build up your knowledge and preferences. There are no rules about what you should drink with what and few Greeks bother about vintages. The relaxed attitude of the Greeks to wine is part of the Greek attitude to food and drink in general. The accent is on enjoyment and conviviality.

Note on the Pronunciation of Greek Words

Accepted spellings of classical Greek names of people and places are used in this book. Modern words, however, are rendered in the transliteration according to their pronunciation in modern demotic Greek. They appear in italics and the acute accent (ˊ) indicates which syllable is stressed.

Although Greek is virtually phonetic, there are problems in rendering Greek letter for letter into Roman letters. For example, *bíra* (beer) would have to be rendered *mpíra*; *anginára* (artichoke) would be *agkinára*; *yaúrti* (yogurt) would be *giaoúrti*, and so on. Since there is as yet no accepted way of transliterating modern Greek into the Roman alphabet, this book keeps this as simple and as near to the original Greek sound as possible.

Visitors to certain parts of Greece will notice differences in pronunciation, though not in spelling. Cretan Greek, for example, softens *k* to *ch* as in *church*. This sound is also heard in Rhodes and Chios, but the differences are not great enough to confuse the foreigner.

To pronounce the Greek words in this book use the following pronunciation guide:

Pronounce a as *a* in *sat*
b as *b* in *bag*
d as *d* in *dig*
dh as *th* in *this*
e as *e* in *wet*
f as *f* in *fish*
g as *g* in *give*
h as *ch* in Scottish *loch*
  or
  as *h* in *human*, before *e* or *i* sounds
i as *ee* in *meet*
k as *k* in *king*
ks as *x* in *fox*

l as *l* in *like*
m as *m* in *miss*
n as *n* in *nice*
o as *ou* in *bought*
p as *p* in *pack*
ps as *ps* in *tips*
r as *r* in *red*, but rolled
s as *s* in *set*
t as *t* in *take*
th as *th* in *think*
u as *oo* in *spoon*
v as *v* in *victory*
y as *y* in *yes*
z as *z* in *zero*

Glossary

alévri flour
amígdhalo almond
anámikto mixed, assorted
anginára artichoke
angúri cucumber
ánitho dill
apó of
araká peas
áspro white
avgó egg
avgolémono egg and lemon
bahári allspice, spice
bámies okra, lady's fingers
bríki long-handled metal coffee
    pot for making Greek coffee
brókolo broccoli
burekákia savoury rolls
dháfni bay
dhendhrolívano rosemary
dhiósmo mint
dholmádhes stuffed vine leaves
domáta tomato
dzadzíki cucumber and yogurt
    dip
eliá olive
ellinikó Greek
fakí dried lentils
faskómilo sage
fasoládha bean soup
fasóli haricot bean, kidney bean
fasulákia green beans
fayí food, meal
féta slice, a white salty cheese
    made from sheep's or goat's
    milk
fíllo fillo pastry, leaf

fitíni cooking medium made from
    olive oil
friganiá toast
frúto fruit
fúrno oven
garífalo cloves
glikániso anise
glikó sweet, jam, sweetmeat
hamomíli camomile
hilopítes noodles
himóna winter
hórto herb, vegetable
húmus chick pea and sesame dip
kafé coffee
kaimáki froth, cream
kaló good
kalokéri summer
kanélla cinnamon
karaméla caramel
karídhi walnut
karóto carrot
kástano chestnut
ke and
kefalotíri a pale yellow, semihard
    salted cheese. Its name refers to
    its head-like (*kefáli*) shape
keftédhes balls, patties
kidhóni quince
kímino cumin
kokkinoyúli beetroot
kolokitháki courgette, zucchini
kolokíthi marrow, pumpkin
kombósta compote
krasí wine
kréma cream, custard
krommídhi onion

kukí broad bean
kunupídhi cauliflower
kurabiédhes shortbread
kurkúti batter
ksídhi vinegar
ksiró dried
ladheró cooked in oil
ládhi oil, olive oil
lahanikó vegetable
láhano cabbage
lemóni lemon
maidanó parsley, coriander leaf
makarónia macaroni, pasta
manitári mushroom
máratho fennel
marúli cos lettuce, long crisp lettuce
mayirihó cooked, clarified (as in clarified butter)
me with
méli honey
melitzána aubergine, eggplant
métrio medium, coffee with a little sugar
mezé, pl. *mezédhes* titbit, snack
mílo apple
mirtiá myrtle
moshokáridho nutmeg
musaká moussaka, a dish made with layers of aubergine slices and topped with a white sauce
mustárdha mustard
nistísimo Lenten (food)
óreksi appetite
orektikó appetizer
ósprio pulse, legume
parthéno virgin
pásta pasta, dough, paste, pastry
pastítsio baked macaroni
patáta potato
pepóni melon
piláfi pilaf rice
piperiá green pepper
pítta cake, pie, bread
pizélia peas
portokáli orange

potó drink, beverage
prásina green
práso leek
psíhula breadcrumbs
psomí bread, loaf
radhíki dandelion
repanáki radish
revíthi chick pea
rígani marjoram, origanum (not to be confused with the herb oregano which is popular in Italian cookery)
rízi rice
rodhákino peach
saganáki frying pan, fried cheese
saláta salad
sáltsa sauce, gravy
sélino celery
sfungáto omelette
síko fig
skéto plain, coffee without sugar
skordhaliá garlic sauce
skórdho garlic
spanáki spinach
spayéto spaghetti
stafíli grape
sto fúrno baked
súpa soup
susámi sesame
tahíni sesame paste
thimári thyme
tiganíta fritter, pancake
tirí cheese
trígono triangle
tsái tea
tsuréki bun, brioche
vasilikó basil
veríkokko apricot
vrastó boiled
vútiro butter
yahní stew
yaúrti yogurt
yemistó stuffed
yíro round, around
záhari sugar
zaharoméno sugared